"Jesus Christ — Son of God"

An Inductive Study
in
The Gospel of John (Part 1)

"AND TRULY JESUS DID MANY OTHER SIGNS IN THE PRESENCE OF HIS
DISCIPLES, WHICH ARE NOT WRITTEN IN THIS BOOK; BUT THESE ARE
WRITTEN THAT YOU MAY BELIEVE THAT JESUS IS THE CHRIST, THE SON
OF GOD, AND THAT BELIEVING YOU MAY HAVE LIFE IN HIS NAME."
JOHN 20:30, 31

Published by Morningstar Christian Chapel
16241 Leffingwell Road
Whittier, California 90603

Background Information

AUTHOR:

John the Apostle, son of Zebedee and Salome, and younger brother of James. Jesus nicknamed John and his brother "Sons of Thunder" (Mark 3:17). John was among the Galileans who followed John the Baptist until they were called to follow Jesus at the beginning of His ministry (John 1:19–51). John was among the twelve men who were selected to be apostles (Luke 6:12–16). After Christ's ascension John became one of the "pillars" of the church in Jerusalem along with James and Peter. He refers to himself in this Gospel as *"the disciple whom Jesus loved"* and may have been the only surviving apostle at the time of the writing. In the latter years of John's life he was banished to Patmos where he received the vision of the future of Jesus Chist recorded for us in the Book of Revelation.

DATE OF WRITING:

Written between 85–90 A.D. from Ephesus, after the destruction of Jerusalem (70 A.D.) and before John's exile to the island of Patmos. According to tradition, John wrote this Gospel from Ephesus.

PURPOSE FOR WRITING:

This book presents the most powerful case in all of the Bible for the deity of the incarnate Son of God. John states his purpose directly in John 20:31.

KEYS TO JOHN:

Key Words: Jesus Christ—Son of God

Key Verse: John 20:31 *"But these are written, that ye might believe that Jesus is the Christ, the Son of God; and that believing ye might have life through His name."*

John

Study Outline

The Picture of Jesus in the Gospel of John

CHAPTER PICTURE

1	The Word (1:1; 14)
	The Lamb of God (1:29; 36)
2	The Temple (2:19)
3	Son of Man (3:13)
4	Living Water (4:10)
5	Son of God 95:19–29)
6	Bread of Life (6:35)
7	The Christ (7:26; 31; 41)
8	I AM (8:58)
9	Light of the World (9:15)
10	Good Shepherd (10:14)
11	Resurrection (11:25)
12	King of Israel (12:13)
13	Servant (13:13–16)
14	Way, Truth, Life (14:6)
15	True Vine (15:1)
16	Overcomer (16:33)
17	Priest praying (17)
18	King of Jews (18:39)
19	Crucified (19:18)
20	Giver of the Holy Spirit 20:22)
21	Lord (21:7)

Lesson Index – part 1

Always begin any Bible Study in prayer. It is the Holy Spirit who teaches us and without Him we are only doing a memory exercise with no spiritual results.

DAY 1—BEGIN IN PRAYER

1. Read the entire Gospel of John. (*You **can** do it*—it is very important to see John's message as a whole even though we will be breaking it down into individual sections.)

2. Read John 1–4. While you are reading underline any verses that the Lord speaks to you through or any that have special meaning to you.

3. Re-read the verses that you underlined.

4. Spend this time in prayer asking the Lord to teach you through the study of His Word.

DAY 2—BEGIN IN PRAYER

1. Read John 1.

2. Re-read John 1:1–18 and record a Title for this section. (Title = five to seven word description that summarizes the section of scripture.)

3. Re-read John 1:19–34 and record a Title for this section.

4. Re-read John 1:35–51 and record a Title for this section.

DAY 3—BEGIN IN PRAYER

1. Read John 2.

2. Re-read John 2:1–11 and record a Title for this section.

3. Re-read John 2:12–25 and record a Title for this section.

DAY 4—BEGIN IN PRAYER

1. Read John 3.

2. Re-read John 3:1–21 and record a Title for this section.

3. Re-read John 3:22–36 and record a Title for this section.

DAY 5—BEGIN IN PRAYER

1. Read John 4.

2. Re-read John 4:1–26 and record a Title for this section.

3. Re-read John 4:27–42 and record a Title for this section.

4. Re-read John 4:43–54 and record a Title for this section.

DAY 6—BEGIN IN PRAYER

1. This time put yourself on the scene. Imagine that you were there—these are real men and women face to face with God in the flesh. Read John 1–4.

    a. What is your reaction?

    b. What is your decision?

    c. What are you willing to sacrifice to follow?

    d. Will you only come at night or will you tell everyone who will listen?

2. Spend some time in prayer about your answers to these questions and others that the Lord may be asking you. He is waiting to hear from your heart.

Study to shew thyself approved unto God, a workman that needeth not to be ashamed, rightly dividing the word of truth.
2 Timothy 2:15

4

DAY 1—BEGIN IN PRAYER

1. Read John 1:1–18.

2. Re-read John 1:1–18. The following terms that are introduced in these first 18 verses are known as *"the prologue."* Underline these terms in the text:
    -The Word   -God
    -Life   -Light
    -Darkness   -Witness
    -Rejection/reception   -Belief
    -Regeneration (becoming a child of God)   -Glory
    -Incarnation (the Word becoming flesh)   -Grace
    -The one and only Son of the Father   -Truth
    -Fullness   -The world

    Note: In the rest of the Gospel, John expands and illustrates each of these terms from Jesus' life and ministry.

3. Write down everything 1:1–18 says about the Word. *(Who and What He is, What He does?)*

4. Choose a verse to memorize this week. Begin working on it now.

DAY 2—BEGIN IN PRAYER

1. Read John 1:1–18.

2. Re-read John 1:1–5.

3. John begins in the *beginning*. (No human genealogy in the Gospel of John.) John parallels the words of the creation account. He stresses that *"the Word"* already existed at the creation account. What more can you learn about *"the beginning"* from the following verses?

   a. Genesis 1:1

   b. Hebrews 1:10

   c. Revelation 1:8

4. John called the Son of God, who was with God His Father in the beginning, the *Word*. As the *Word*, the Son of God fully conveys and communicates God. What more do these scriptures teach us about the *Word*?

   a. 1 John 1:1–3

   b. 1 John 5:6, 7

   c. Colossians 1:13–17

d. Revelation 19:11–13

5.   In verse 4 John tells us, *"In Him was life; and the life was the light of men." "Life"* is a key theme in John's Gospel; it is used thirty-six times. Creation needs to receive life from *"the Word"*—for He is the source of life. The word used here is always used to describe the divine, eternal life. Find out more about the source of life.

a. John 6:33–35

b. John 14:6

c. Colossians 3:3, 4

d. 1John 5:10–13

6.   What specific lessons did you learn today? *(Truths to depend on; promises to believe; warnings to heed.)*

7.   Write these lessons in the form of a question to yourself. *(What should I do? What should I not be doing? Do I truly believe these truths?)*

DAY 3—BEGIN IN PRAYER

1. Read John 1:1–18.

2. Re-read John 1:6–11.

3. *"There was a man sent from God,"* his ministry was to be a witness of the coming of the Light. *"He was **not** the Light,"* What do we learn about this John from the following references?

    a. Malachi 3:1

    b. Matthew 11:7–11

    c. Luke 1:13–17

    d. Luke 1:76–78

4. Light and darkness are another recurring theme in John's Gospel. God is light while Satan is *"the power of darkness."* People love either the light or the darkness, and this love controls their actions. What more can we learn about this truth?

    a. John 3:19, 20

    b. John 8:12

c. Romans 13:12–14

d. Ephesians 5:8–14

5. Jesus, the Creator and Savior *"was in the world, and the world was made by Him, and the world knew Him not."* Jesus, the *True Light* suffered rejection from the world but this reaction did not come as a surprise to Him. Read and meditate on the extent and depth of love God has for you.

a. Isaiah 53 (Whole chapter.)

6. What specific lessons did you learn today? *(Truths to depend on; promises to believe; warnings to heed; examples to follow/not follow.)*

7. Write these lessons in the form of a question to yourself. *(What should I do? What should I not be doing? Do I truly believe these Truths? Do I need to make any changes?)*

DAY 4—BEGIN IN PRAYER *(Don't forget!)*

1. Read John 1:1–18.

2. Re-read John 1:12–14.

3. Though the rejection of Christ was universal, individuals did respond personally. The Greek word translated *"received"* is used in the sense of accepting. To receive Jesus is to welcome and acknowledge Him as Savior and Lord. And in doing so God has given us the power (privilege, permission) to become the sons and daughters of God. Study this awesome privilege and the responsibility that goes with it.

    a. Romans 8:12–15

    b. 2Corinthians 6:14–18

    c. Galatians 3:26–29

    d. 2Peter 1:3, 4

    Personal: Have you personally received Jesus Christ as your Savior and Lord? This Bible Study will make no difference in your life now or in eternity if you do not know Him. You must understand that there is no way for you to meet the standard of perfection that is required to enter into the presence of the Holy God. Therefore, because of God's love for us He sent His Son Jesus, (He became flesh and dwelt among man) He died on the cross paying the penalty for our sins (past, present, and future). He rose from the dead and now lives forever making intercession for us. Now is the day of salvation (2Corinthians 6:2) Ask Him into your heart today.

4. According to verse 13, how do we become children of God?
    See Ephesians 2:8, 9 and John 15:16.

5. Look up the definition of the following words from verse 14 for a better understanding of their meaning? *(Use a Bible Dictionary, Vine's Dictionary of New Testament Words, Strong's Concordance, or if you do not have access to the above, use a regular English Language Dictionary.)*

a. The Word

b. Flesh

c. Dwelt

d. Beheld

e. Glory

f. Grace

g. Truth

6. What specific lessons did you learn today? *(Truths to depend on; promises to believe; warnings to heed; examples to follow / not follow.)*

7. Write these lessons in the form of a question to yourself. *(What should I do? What should I not be doing? Do I truly believe these truths? Do I need to make any changes?)*

DAY 5—BEGIN IN PRAYER

1.   Read John 1:1–18.

2.   Re-read John 1:15–18.

3.   Jesus was full of grace and truth, this is His nature and by union with Him all His perfection and righteousness became ours. What more can we learn about our relationship to Christ?

   a. 1Corinthians 1:30, 31

   b. Ephesians 4:13, 14

   c. Philippians 1:9–11

   d. Philippians 3:7–9

4.   The Law was given by Moses, it was not a system of grace, nor could it make men perfect. What was the purpose of the Law? What happened to the Law when Jesus came?

   a. Romans 3:20

   b. Galatians 3:24, 25

c. Hebrews 10:1–4

d. Matthew 5:17, 18

5. In verse 18 it says: *"No man has seen God at any time. The only begotten Son— He declares Him to us."* The word *"declares"* means: *to explain; to unfold; to lead the way.* Jesus Christ explains God to us and interprets Him for us. We simply cannot understand God apart from knowing His Son, Jesus Christ. Find out more about this truth in the following verses.

a. Matthew 11:27

b. Colossians 1:14, 15

c. Colossians 1:19

d. Colossians 2:9, 10

6. What specific lessons did you learn today? *(Truths to depend on; promises to believe; warnings to heed; examples to follow/not follow.)*

7.   Write these lessons in the form of a question to yourself. *(What should I do? What should I not be doing? Do I truly believe these truths? Do I need to make any changes?)*

DAY 6—BEGIN IN PRAYER

1.   Read John 1:1–18. *(It's important!)*

2.   What specific lessons has the Lord taught you this week?

3.   Have you memorized the verse you chose? *(Complete it today.)*

> *Thy Word have I hid in mine heart, that I might not sin against Thee. Psalms 119:11*

4.   Do you truly believe that Jesus is God? Because He created all, including you, and He holds your very life in His hands, can you trust Him with it? With your families' lives? *"In Him is Life and Light."* Do you love the Light? Do you recognize the privilege of being called a *"child of God"*? You can behold His glory and be filled with His grace and truth. Are you? Today is the day to allow Him to make these changes in your heart and your actions, ask Him now in prayer.

> *And the Word was made flesh, and dwelt among us, (and we beheld His glory, the glory as of the only begotten of the Father,) full of grace and truth. John 1:14*

DAY 1—BEGIN IN PRAYER

1. Read John 1:19–34.

2. John the Apostle never names himself in his Gospel; the name "John" always refers to John the Baptist. Re-read John 1:6–8 and 19–34. Who or what did John the Baptist say he was? How did he describe himself?

3. What did John the Baptist testify about Jesus? List as many observations as you can find in verses 19–34.

4. Choose a verse to memorize this week. Begin working on it now. *(Tape it to the dash of your car, or on your bathroom mirror.)*

DAY 2—BEGIN IN PRAYER

1. Read John 1:19–34.

2. Re-read John 1:19–23. *(No Cheating!)*

3. Verse 19 begins, *"Now this is the testimony of John (the Baptist)."* What was his testimony? *"He was not the Light."* When challenged, John had the answers to the questions. It was his calling to bear witness to the Light. What is our calling as Christians to this generation?

    a. Matthew 5:14–16

    b. 2Corinthians 3:5, 6 *(Use a modern version if possible.)*

c. 2Corinthians 5:20

d. Ephesians 5:8

4. How are we to respond when we are questioned about our calling?

a. Psalms 40:8–10

b. 1Peter 3:15

c. Colossians 4:5, 6

d. 2Timothy 2:24, 25

5. We are called to bear witness of the Light. We are not able to help or save anyone. We are to direct them to Jesus as He is the One who brings Life. We need to be careful to be faithful to our calling and be sure that we never forget that we are only *"a voice"* to point the world to Jesus. What blessings and warnings do we find in the following verses to the faithful servant?

a. Matthew 25:21

b. Hebrews 6:10

c. Proverbs 29:23

d. James 4:10

6. What specific lessons did you learn today? *(Truths to depend on; promises to believe; warnings to heed; examples to follow.)*

7. Write these lessons in the form of a question to yourself. *(What should I do? What should I not be doing? Do I truly believe these truths?)*

DAY 3—BEGIN IN PRAYER

1. Read John 1:19–34.

2. Re-read John 1:24–28.

3. The title of *Pharisee* meant *separated ones*. They separated themselves from lax religious practices and lived strictly by the Law. However, in order to avoid breaking the Law, they had minutely defined the precise ways each law must be kept in every conceivable situation leading to spiritual pride and external religion. What description is given of the scribes and Pharisees and why?

a. Matthew 3:7

b. Matthew 23:13–15

c. Matthew 23:23–25

d. Matthew 23:27–29

4.   Read Matthew 5:20. How can *"your righteousness exceed the righteousness of the scribes and the Pharisees"*?

a. 1Corinthians 1:30

b. 2Corinthians 5:21

c. Romans 5:19–21

d. Philippians 3:8, 9

5.   John was questioned regarding his baptizing and he pointed out that he merely baptized with water which was a symbolic act of repentance and that he was only pointing the way to the One who would truly forgive sin. It is

very important that we never forget who we are serving and begin to act in pride. John told His accusers, *"there stands One among you...whose shoe latchet I am not worthy to unloose."* What can we learn about our attitude before the Lord in serving Him?

a. Psalm 34:18

b. Psalm 51:17

c. Isaiah 57:15

d. Isaiah 66:1, 2

6.   What specific lessons did you learn today? *(Truths to depend on; promises to believe; warnings to heed; examples to follow.)*

7.   Write these lessons in the form of a question to yourself. *(What should I do? What should I not be doing? Do I truly believe these truths?)*

DAY 4—BEGIN IN PRAYER

1. Read John 1:19–34.

2. Re-read John 1:29–31.

3. John pointed to Jesus and used a title, *"Lamb of God,"* that would be associated in the minds of the Jews with the Passover Lamb. Research this through the scriptures so that you will better understand the meaning.

    a. Genesis 4:4

    b. Exodus 12:1–14 *(Don't try to write this all down.)*

    c. 1 Corinthians 5:7, 8

4. John tells us, by example the most important point we must make when seeking to tell others about Jesus — *"Behold, the Lamb of God, which takes away the sins of the world."* John knew who God was and he declared Him openly. How did Jesus make this truth clear in His teaching?

    a. John 6:43, 44

    b. John 8:28

c. John 10:27–30

d. John 14:6

5   John had been sent baptizing with water that the Messiah might be revealed to Israel. Read about those who were faithfully awaiting the coming of the Messiah. *Are you?*

a. Luke 2:25, 26

b. Luke 2:36-38

c. Mark 15:43

d. John 8:56 *(Challenge: When did this occur?)*

6.   What specific lessons did you learn today? *(Truths to depend on; promises to believe; warnings to heed; examples to follow.)*

7.   Write these lessons in the form of a question to yourself. *(What should I do? What should I not be doing? Do I truly believe these truths?)*

DAY 5—BEGIN IN PRAYER

1. Read John 1:19–34.

2. Re-read John 1:32–34.

3. John had been told of a sign *"Upon whom thou shalt see the Spirit descending, and remaining on Him, the same is He which baptizeth with the Holy Ghost."* Study the account of Jesus' Baptism in the other Gospels. What additional facts do you find?

   a. Matthew 3:13–17

   b. Mark 1:9–11

   c. Luke 3:21, 22

4. In well-known prophetic passages, the Messiah was depicted as having *"the Spirit descending, and remaining on Him."* See how this would have been a sign to John that would cause him to proclaim, *"this is the Son of God."*

   a. Isaiah 11:1–5

   b. Isaiah 42:1–4

   c. Isaiah 61:1–3

5. Jesus being fully God and fully man lived and ministered by the power of the Holy Spirit.

   Who, being in the form of God, thought it not robbery to be equal with God: But made Himself of no reputation, and took upon Him the form of a servant, and was made in the likeness of men. Philippians 2:6, 7 KJV

   And we, His children, are to live our lives in the same manner. God loves His children and promises to pour out upon each of them the gift of the Holy Spirit in fullness so that they may have power to enjoy an abundant and fruitful life. The question was asked of some followers in the book of Acts *"Have you received the Spirit since you believed?" Acts 19:2. Have you?* Here's what the Bible says about Baptism of the Holy Spirit.

   a. Acts 2:17 and 39

   b. Acts 1:8

   c. John 7:37–39

   d. Luke 11:9 and 13

   e. Acts 2:4 and 33

6. What specific lessons did you learn today? *(Truths to depend on; promises to believe; warnings to heed; examples to follow.)*

7.   Write these lessons in the form of a question to yourself. *(What should I do? What should I not be doing? Do I truly believe these truths?)*

DAY 6—BEGIN IN PRAYER *(Don't neglect to seek Him.)*

1.   Read John 1:19–34.

2.   Did you memorize the verse you chose? *Finish it today!*

3.   How has the Lord specifically spoken to you this week? Is there any area where change is required? Do it today. Have you been that faithful voice pointing the way to the Messiah? Are you trying to be a witness by your own power or through the power of the Holy Spirit?

The next day John seeth Jesus coming unto him, and saith, Behold the Lamb of God, which taketh away the sin of the world.
John 1:29

DAY 1—BEGIN IN PRAYER

1. Read John 1:35–51.

2. How would you describe Jesus from what He says and does in:

    a. John 1:37–39

    b. John 1:42–43

    c. John 1:47–51

3. What did each of the following men discover about Jesus and how did they discover this?

    a. Andrew and the other disciple (vs. 35–39)

    b. Andrew's brother Simon (vs. 40–42)

    c. Philip (vs. 43–45)

    d. Nathanael (vs. 45–50)

Jesus CHRIST son of GOD

4.   Choose a verse to memorize this week. *Begin working on it now.*

DAY 2—BEGIN IN PRAYER

1.   Read John 1:35–51.

2.   Re-read John 1:35–39.

3.   This section of the Gospel of John records how the first believers came to follow Jesus. The progression provides an excellent example for us to follow. John the Baptist was to point to the Light. He saw Jesus, pointed Him out and his disciples left and followed Jesus. When they heard, they chose to follow and their lives would forever be changed.

*Personal: When you heard, did you make a **decision** to follow?*

How has following changed your life?

What direction and promises are given to those who follow in these verses?

a. Matthew 4:19

b. Matthew 16:24–26

c. John 12:26

d. 2Timothy 4:8

e. James 1:12

4.   Jesus asked them, *"What seek ye?"* It is very important the we check our motives for following Him. Are we looking for eternal life, forgiveness, peace, rest, fulfillment, love—all these and much more are found in Jesus. Learn who Jesus says He is by researching the following Scriptures.

a. John 4:25, 26

b. John 6:35

c. John 9:5

d. John 10:7–11

e. John 11:25

f. John 14:6

g. John 15:1–4

h. Revelation 1:8

5. *Personal: Jesus asks you, "What seek ye?" Is it the Messiah, the Savior? Or were you looking for other things: coming with the wrong motives, hoping to gain, profit or benefit? His offer still stands: "Come and see..."*

6. What specific lessons did you learn today? *(Truths to depend on; promises to believe; warnings to heed; examples to follow.)*

7. Write these lessons in the form of a question to yourself. *(What should I do? What should I not be doing? Do I truly believe these truths?)*

DAY 3—BEGIN IN PRAYER

1. Read John 1:35–51.

2. Re-read John 1:40–42.

3. One of the men that had heard John and followed Jesus was Andrew. (The other is commonly believed to be John—the author of this Gospel.) See what more you can learn about Andrews' life.

   a. John 6:8–10

b. John 12:20–22

c. Matthew 4:18, 19

d. Matthew 10:2–4

4. The result of dwelling with Jesus is recorded for us in these verses. After meeting Jesus, Andrew went directly to find his brother to tell him of the Messiah. When we have Good News we are compelled to share it. What is our privilege and responsibility to those who do not know Jesus?

a. Proverbs 11:30

b. Daniel 12:3

c. Luke 10:2, 3

d. 1Corinthians 9:19–23

5. This desire to reach the lost ought to be burning in our hearts. Yet, unfortunately, we sometimes become complacent to the urgency with which we need to share the Gospel. Use these verses as a reminder of our responsibility to proclaim the way of salvation.

a. Psalm 103:15–18

b. Romans 13:11–14

c. 1 Corinthians 7:29–31

d. 1 Peter 4:7

Doest thou live close by them, or meet them in the streets, or labour with them, or travel with them, or sit and talk with them, and say nothing to them of their souls, or life to come? If their houses were on fire, thou wouldst run and help them; and wilt thou not help them when their souls are almost at the fire of hell?
—*Richard Baxter*

6. What specific lessons did you learn today? *(Truths to depend on; promises to believe; warnings to heed; examples to follow.)*

7. Write these lessons in the form of a question to yourself. *(What should I do? What should I not be doing? Do I truly believe these truths?)*

DAY 4—BEGIN IN PRAYER

1. Read John 1:35–51. *(It's very important!)*

2. Re-read John 1:43–46.

3.   Jesus went forth to Galilee (locate this area on a Bible map) and found Philip.
      Jesus said unto him, *"Follow Me."* The Gospel is spread in many ways, but
      ultimately it is God Who reveals Himself to us through the Holy Spirit. Find
      out more about His calling on our hearts.

      a. John 6:44

      b. John 15:16–19

      c. 2Thessalonians 2:13

      d. 1Peter 2:9

4.   Immediately, Philip found Nathanael saying, *"We have found m, of Whom
      Moses in the law, and the prophets, did write..."* Learn more about the Messiah
      from these prophecies which were well known to Philip and Nathanael.

      a. Genesis 49:10

      b. Isaiah 7:14

      c. Isaiah 9:6, 7

d. Isaiah 28:16

e. Zechariah 12:10

Challenge: These are only a few of many prophecies concerning our Lord's birth, life, death, resurrection and second coming. Use a Concordance or Topical Bible and research this subject further.

5. We learn a very important lesson from Philip as he seeks to bring Nathanael to Jesus. Nathanael is skeptical and rather than arguing with him, Philip simply offers the invitation, *"Come and see."* It is not our responsibility to save, only to faithfully point others in the right direction. What do we learn from these verses?

a. Matthew 5:16

b. 2Corinthians 5:18, 19

c. Colossians 4:6

d. 1Peter 3:15

6. What specific lessons did you learn today? *(Truths to depend on; promises to believe; warnings to heed; examples to follow.)*

7. Write these lessons in the form of a question to yourself. *(What should I do? What should I not be doing? Do I truly believe these truths?)*

DAY 5—BEGIN IN PRAYER *(Don't Forget!)*

1. Read John 1:35–51.

2. Re-read John 1:47–51.

3. Jesus knew Nathanael before He ever met him. He knew his character, his heart, and his actions. In the same way, He knows you, loves you and longs for you to come to Him. What encouragement do you get from the following Scriptures?

    a. Psalm 139:13–17

    b. Isaiah 44:24

    c. Jeremiah 1:5

d. Jeremiah 31:3

4. Here Jesus reveals His omniscience (all-knowing) to Nathanael. Jesus had been aware of Nathanael's exact location before Philip called him. According to Jewish tradition, the expression *"to sit under the fig tree,"* was a term meaning to meditate and study the Scriptures. In verse 51, Jesus used a description that may very well have been very familiar to a student of the Scriptures. Read Genesis 28:10–22 and record your findings regarding *"Jacob's Ladder"* and Jesus.

5. *"Son of man"* was one of our Lord's favorite titles for Himself; it is used eighty-three times in the Gospels and at least thirteen times in John. The title speaks of both the deity and humanity of Jesus. The vision in Daniel 7:13 presents the *"Son of man"* in a definite Messianic setting. Use a Bible Dictionary or Concordance and find as many references to the *"Son of man"* as you have time for. What are a few facts you have learned about the *"Son of man"*?

6. What specific lessons did you learn today? *(Truths to depend on; promises to believe; warnings to heed; examples to follow.)*

7. Write these lessons in the form of a question to yourself. *(What should I do? What should I not be doing? Do I truly believe these truths?)*

DAY 6—BEGIN IN PRAYER

1. Read John 1:35–51.

2. Have you memorized the verse that you chose this week. Make sure that you do it today.

3. Is there a particular area that the Lord is dealing with you in this week? Do not allow the enemy to intervene. *"Resist the devil and he will flee."* When the Lord called you to *"Follow Him"* have you been doing it whole-heartedly? Have you faithfully pointed the way to those who are lost in darkness? Have you called your brother, sister, or neighbor with the invitation *"Come and see..."*? Today would be the very best day.

Nathanael answered and saith unto Him, Rabbi, Thou art the Son of God; thou art the King of Israel. John 1:49

DAY 1—BEGIN IN PRAYER

1. Read John 2:1–11.

2. The word translated *miracles* in verse 11 means: *a sign, mark, or token.* A sign is something that points beyond itself. It teaches a spiritual truth; it points to God and His provision in Jesus. How did Jesus' first miracle (sign) affect His disciples?

3. Think about the purpose of a sign. What does this particular sign reveal about Jesus' character, identity, and mission?

4. Choose a verse to memorize this week. Begin working on it now.

DAY 2—BEGIN IN PRAYER

1. Read John 2:1–11.

2. Re-read John 2:1, 2.

3. On the third day (after Nathanael's call) Jesus and the disciples attended a wedding. A wedding celebration could last as long as a week in those days. The very presence of our Lord gives us an indication that Jesus honors and sanctifies the wedding ceremony and the marriage vow. What can we learn about marriage from the following verses?

    a. Matthew 19:3–9

    b. Romans 7:2

    c. Ephesians 5:31

d. Hebrews 13:4a

4. In the Old Testament we find a beautiful picture of the wedding feast and its relation to the coming of the Messiah. And in the New Testament the truth of the Bridegroom (Jesus) and the bride (the church). Research the following Scriptures and record what you learn about the Bridegroom and the bride.

a. Isaiah 62:4, 5

b. Hosea 2:19, 20

c. Matthew 9:14, 15

d. 2Corinthians 11:2

e. Revelation 19:7

5. The "Life Application Bible" reminds us that Jesus was on a mission to save the world, the greatest mission of mankind. Yet He took time to attend a wedding and take part in its festivities. What example is there for us to follow from His life? Can we serve Him in every part of our lives? Give some specific examples from your life.

6.   What specific lessons did you learn today? *(Truths to depend on; promises to believe; warnings to heed; examples to follow.)*

7.   Write these lessons in the form of a question to yourself. *(What should I do? What should I not be doing? Do I truly believe these truths?)*

DAY 3—BEGIN IN PRAYER *(Call on the Teacher.)*

1.   Read John 2:1–11.

2.   Re-read John 2:3–5.

3.   When a need arose at the wedding, Jesus' mother came to Jesus to have the need met. What can we learn about Mary from the following verses?

     a. Luke 1:26–38

     b. Luke 2:19

     c. John 19:25

d. Acts 1:14

4. Some say that Mary's request may have been more than simply to provide wine. It may have been that Mary desired Jesus to reveal to the guests at this home town wedding what she knew to be true about Him but had been concealed for these many years. His reply of, *"Mine hour is not yet come,"* gives us a clue to the possibility of this hope. *"My hour"* is a term frequently used by Jesus during His ministry. What more do you learn from the following references?

a. John 7:30

b. John 12:23

c. John 13:1

d. John 17:1

5. We would do well to always follow the direction that Mary gave to the servants, *"Whatsoever He says unto you, do it."* Obedience is a sign of a true relationship with the Lord. What direction and encouragement do you get from these Scriptures?

a. 1Samuel 15:22

b. Jeremiah 7:23

c. Romans 6:16

d. 1 John 2:3–5

6. What specific lessons did you learn today? *(Truths to depend on; promises to believe; warnings to heed; examples to follow.)*

7. Write these lessons in the form of a question to yourself. *(What should I do? What should I not be doing? Do I truly believe these truths?)*

DAY 4—BEGIN IN PRAYER

1. Read John 2:1–11. *(Think about it as you read.)*

2. Re-read John 2:6–8.

3. Jesus used ordinary servants to assist in accomplishing this first sign. He often used servants or His followers in the process of working miracles. He could have easily filled the stone waterpots with wine, yet He graciously includes us in His working. Look up the following verses and see how you and I can be used by the Lord to bring Him honor and glory.

a. Acts 9:13–17

b. Ephesians 2:10

c. 2Timothy 2:21

d. 1Peter 1:6–9

4. *"The servants filled the waterpots to the brim."* They did their very best in this service and likewise so should we in our service for the Lord. What direction do we receive regarding the diligence with which we are to serve?

a. Ephesians 6:6–8

b. Colossians 3:17

c. 1Thessalonians 5:18

d. 1Peter 4:11

5. Jesus used a symbol of the old—the stone waterpots, after the manner of purifying—to begin to show forth the new. How are we, as believers, purified?

a. Psalm 51:10–12

b. Psalm 130:3, 4

c. Acts 5:30, 31

d. Colossians 2:13–15

6.   What specific lessons did you learn today? *(Truths to depend on; promises to believe; warnings to heed; examples to follow.)*

7.   Write these lessons in the form of a question to yourself. *(What should I do? What should I not be doing? Do I truly believe these truths?)*

DAY 5—BEGIN IN PRAYER

1.   Read John 2:1–11.

2.   Re-read John 2:9–11.

3. Some may use this first miracle of Jesus as license to drink wine or other alcoholic beverages. This is not the context of this scripture and tradition is far different today. Use the following verses in making a decision regarding use of alcoholic drinks.

    a. Proverbs 20:1

    b. Luke 21:34

    c. 1 Peter 4:3, 4

    d. Romans 14:13–21

4. Wine was a symbol of joy and a central part of the messianic wedding banquet (Isaiah 25:6). How does Jesus use the analogy of wine in Luke 5:37, 38 and what parallel do you see with this first miracle at Cana?

5. The result of this first miracle was that the disciples believed Him. This was a strengthening of their belief and as they spent more time with the Lord their faith would grow stronger and stronger. And so it must be with us, we cannot grow in faith if we do not invest our time and energy in spending time with Him, learning of Him, and doing the things He directs us to do. How do these verses remind you of your need for intimate fellowship with the Lord?

    a. Psalm 25:14

b. Jeremiah 33:3

c. Matthew 11:28–30

d. Matthew 16:24–26

e. John 15:15

6. What specific lessons did you learn today? *(Truths to depend on; promises to believe; warnings to heed; examples to follow.)*

7. Write these lessons in the form of a question to yourself. *(What should I do? What should I not be doing? Do I truly believe these truths?)*

DAY 6—BEGIN IN PRAYER

1. Read John 2:1–11.

2. What specific lessons has the Lord taught you this week? Are you faithfully serving Him and representing Him wherever He takes you? Are you expecting Him to be who you desire rather than who He is? Are you doing *"whatsoever He tells you"*? Is your daily fellowship with Jesus causing your faith in Him to increase?

The servants at the wedding in Cana were faithfully serving and they found themselves in the place where God does miracles. It will be the same for us today.

This beginning of miracles did Jesus in Cana of Galilee, and manifested forth His glory; and His disciples believed on Him. John 2:11

DAY 1—BEGIN IN PRAYER

1. Read John 2:12–25.

2. Read Exodus 12 and Deuteronomy 16:14. What was the reason for the celebration of Passover? And who was required to attend this feast?

3. Re-read John 2:12–25 trying to put yourself in the shoes of the disciples or a poor, sincere worshipper of God. What might your reaction be to Jesus cleansing the Temple?

4. Choose a verse to memorize this week. *Begin working on it now.*

DAY 2—BEGIN IN PRAYER

1. Read John 2:12–25.

2. Re-read John 2:12–13.

3. Use a Bible Map and locate the city of Capernaum. Where is it located? What body of water is very near this city?

    What more can you learn about this city that was Jesus' home base for ministry in this area?

    a. Matthew 4:13–17

    b. Matthew 8:5–10

c. Matthew 17:24–27

d. Matthew 11:21–24

4. The people of Capernaum were condemned for their unbelief. What truths and warnings are we given in these Scriptures regarding *unbelief?*

a. Matthew 13:57, 58

b. Matthew 17:19, 20

c. Mark 9:24

d. Mark 16:14

e. Hebrews 3:12

5. The reference to Jesus' brethren in verse 12 refers to His actual half brothers and sisters. See what more you can learn about them?

a. Matthew 12:46

b. Mark 6:3

c. Acts 1:14

d. Galatians 1:19

6.   What specific lessons did you learn today? *(Truths to depend on; promises to believe; warnings to heed; examples to follow.)*

7.   Write these lessons in the form of a question to yourself. *(What should I do? What should I not be doing? Do I truly believe these truths?)*

DAY 3—BEGIN IN PRAYER *(Don't forget.)*

1.   Read John 2:12–25.

2.   Re-read John 2:14–17.

3.   God had originally instructed the people of Israel to bring an animal for sacrifice from their own flocks. But, the temple priests had set up a place where those who came from a far distance could purchase an animal for sacrifice. This may have begun as a well-intentioned convenience but by

this time was a source of great income for many who only desired to exploit those who came to the temple. Also, they had set up shop in the Court of the Gentiles, so that those who came to worship would find it nearly impossible. Worship and edification needs to and *must be* the reason that we attend church. What direction do we find regarding the purity with which we are to seek the Lord?

a. 1Chronicles 29:17

b. 1Samuel 12:24

c. Isaiah 66:1, 2

d. Isaiah 29:13–16

4.   As Christians, we need to be very careful to keep our lives pure from sin and the influences of the world that would defile our worship and dim the witness that we are to be to the world. What reminders do we find regarding our purity of heart?

a. Psalm 24:3, 4

b. Matthew 5:8

c. Philippians 1:9, 10

d. Philippians 2:14–16

5. Psalm 69 refers not only to the Psalmist but is a prophecy regarding the coming Messiah. Read Psalm 69:4–9 and record what you find that relates to the Lord Jesus Christ.

6. What specific lessons did you learn today? *(Truths to depend on; promises to believe; warnings to heed; examples to follow.)*

7. Write these lessons in the form of a question to yourself. *(What should I do? What should I not be doing? Do I truly believe these truths?)*

DAY 4—BEGIN IN PRAYER

1. Read John 2:12–25. *(It will become part of your life.)*

2. Re-read John 2:18–22.

3. There was still a godly remnant in Israel who loved God and revered His temple, but most of the religious leaders were false shepherds who exploited the people. When Jesus cleansed the temple, He "declared war" on the hypocritical religious leaders. Research the following references and see what Jesus thinks of hypocrites.

a. Matthew 6:2, 5, 16

b. Matthew 7:1–5

c. Matthew 23:13–15

d. Matthew 23:23–28

4. The Jews sought a sign and the sign that Jesus gave them was His death and resurrection. Because of the hardness of their hearts they did not see or understand His proof of His authority to cleanse *"His Father's House."* The death and resurrection is the only truth on which we need to stand when witnessing to those who "look for a sign." What do you learn about the resurrection from the following verses?

a. Matthew 12:40

b. Mark 8:31

c. 1 Corinthians 15:14

d. 1 Corinthians 15:17–21

5.   The temple was an important element of the Jewish faith, for in it God was supposed to dwell. Jesus' statement about destroying this temple actually predicted the end of the Jewish religious system. Instead of worship in the temple, those who desired to worship would need to come to Jesus. The New Testament speaks of the temple, where is it? What do we learn about caring for it?

   a. 1Corinthians 3:16, 17

   b. 1Corinthians 6:19, 20

   c. 2Corinthians 6:16

   d. Ephesians 2:19–22

6.   What specific lessons did you learn today? *(Truths to depend on; promises to believe; warnings to heed; examples to follow.)*

7.   Write these lessons in the form of a question to yourself. *(What should I do? What should I not be doing? Do I truly believe these truths?)*

DAY 5—BEGIN IN PRAYER

1. Read John 2:12–25.

2. Re-read John 2:23–25.

3. While in Jerusalem for the Passover, Jesus performed miracles that are not given in detail in any of the Gospels. Because of the miracles, many people professed to believe in Him; but Jesus did not accept their profession. Its one thing to respond to a miracle, it is quite another thing to commit oneself to Jesus Christ and *"continue in His Word."* What fruit is evident in the life of the one who believes and truly is saved?

    a. John 8:30, 31

    b. John 15:4–9

    c. Hebrews 3:12–14

    d. James 1:25

4. Jesus knew what was in the heart of those who followed Him. They were following for the wrong motives—for pride, selfishness, and gain. What do you learn from this man who was following Jesus for the wrong motives? What counsel was given by Peter to correct this wrong heart attitude?

    Simon the sorcerer — Acts 8:9–24

5.   Jesus knew the hearts of those who followed Him. Record what you learn from each of the following incidents.

a. Mark 2:6–12

b. Mark 3:1–6

c. Mark 8:14–21

Personal: Now read and meditate on Hebrews 4:12, 13. What is the Lord saying to you about the state of your heart toward Him?

6.   What specific lessons did you learn today? *(Truths to depend on; promises to believe; warnings to heed; examples to follow.)*

7.   Write these lessons in the form of a question to yourself. *(What should I do? What should I not be doing? Do I truly believe these truths?)*

DAY 6—BEGIN IN PRAYER

1. Read John 2:12–25.

2. Is there any area that the Lord has been specifically dealing with you about this week? *"Do not grieve the Holy Spirit"* by putting off this change or action. What is the condition of your heart? What are your reasons for following Him? Are they purely for worship and praise?

3. Have you memorized your verse for the week? *Finish it today!*

Jesus answered and said unto them, destroy this Temple, and in three days I will raise it up. John 2:19

DAY 1—BEGIN IN PRAYER

1. Read John 3:1–21.

2. Read John 3:1–21 again, recording all the facts you learn about the following:

   a. Kingdom of God

   b. Born again, Born of the Spirit

   c. Everlasting life

3. Research the subject of the Kingdom of God by looking up each of the following references and listing all that you find.

   a. Matthew 4:17

   b. Matthew 5:10–12

c. Matthew 7:21

d. Luke 4:43

e. Luke 12:31

f. Luke 13:22–30

4.   Choose a verse to memorize this week. *Begin working on it now.*

DAY 2—BEGIN IN PRAYER

1.   Read John 3:1–21.

2.   Re-read John 3:1–8.

3.   Nicodemus, a Pharisee, a ruler of the Jews (member of the Jewish supreme court—the Sanhedrin), came to Jesus at night maybe out of fear of being seen or maybe because of the tremendous crowds in the day. He was seeking answers, he had also seen the miracles. What he'd learn would eventually change his life. What other details do you learn about this man, Nicodemus?

a. John 7:45–53

b. John 19:38–42

4. Look up the definition of the following words to find more about their meaning. *(Use a Bible Dictionary, Vine's Dictionary of New Testament Words, Strong's Concordance, or a regular English Language Dictionary.)*

   a. Rabbi (v. 2)

   b. Born Again (v. 3)

   c. Kingdom of God (v. 3)

   d. Spirit (v. 6)

5. Nicodemus had come to Jesus and immediately Jesus gave him the answer to man's deepest need, the need for salvation. *"Except a man* (every man—rich or poor; bond or free; powerful or powerless; religious or heathen) *be born from above, he cannot see the kingdom of God."* This spiritual birth comes through the Word of God and by the Spirit of God. What more can you learn about this new birth?

   a. Ezekiel 36:26

   b. Romans 8:1–4

   c. 2Corinthians 5:17

d. Ephesians 1:3–7

"The new life begotten by the Spirit of God is as mysterious as the wind. That Spirit, bearing the germ of a new life, rejoices to enter each open casement and to fill each vacuum, wherever one allows it." —F.B. Meyer

6. What specific lessons did you learn today? *(Truths to depend on; promises to believe; warnings to heed; examples to follow.)*

7. Write these lessons in the form of a question to yourself. *(What should I do? What should I not be doing? Do I truly believe these truths?)*

DAY 3—BEGIN IN PRAYER

1. Read John 3:1–21. *(It is very necessary. How are you doing on your memory verse?)*

2. Re-read John 3:9–15.

3. Nicodemus' response was the same as every man when he seeks to understand spiritual truth with the natural mind. What do we learn about man's inability to understand the truths of God?

    a. Romans 8:5–8

b. 1Corinthians 1:18

c. 1Corinthians 2:14

d. 2Corinthians 4:4

4. It is the work of the Holy Spirit to teach, instruct and guide the believer. When we have turned from our sins in repentance and accepted Jesus Christ as our Savior and Lord, then what help will we receive from the Holy Spirit?

a. Ezekiel 36:27, 28

b. John 14:16, 17

c. John 14:26, 27

d. 1John 2:27

5. Jesus gave the first illustration of the wind, now He gives Nicodemus another. Herein is eternal life, *"as Moses lifted up the serpent in the wilderness, even so must the Son of Man be lifted up."* To be *"lifted up"* in Jesus' time was a euphemism for death on the cross. Read the account of Moses and the Israelites in Numbers 21:4–9 and compare it with John 8:28 and John 12:32–34, what similarities to you find?

Personal: What is the future for those who believe in Him who was lifted up? Do you believe? If you do then your future is certain?

6. What specific lessons did you learn today? *(Truths to depend on; promises to believe; warnings to heed; examples to follow.)*

7. Write these lessons in the form of a question to yourself. *(What should I do? What should I not be doing? Do I truly believe these truths?)*

DAY 4—BEGIN IN PRAYER

1. Read John 3:1–21.

2. Re-read John 3:16–18.

3. John 3:16, along with the rest of the New Testament, tells us that apart from God's intervention, people perish. Look up the following Scriptures to confirm this truth.

   a. Luke 13:1–5

   b. John 10:25–28

c. Romans 2:12

d. 1Corinthians 1:18

e. 2Peter 3:9

4.   Look up the definition of the following words for a deeper understanding of their meaning.

     a. Loved (v. 16)

     b. Whosoever (v. 16)

     c. Believeth (v. 16)

     d. Perish (v. 16)

     e. Everlasting (v. 16)

5. The mission of the Son was to save those who were lost (which, as we have learned, was everyone). What more can we learn about this mission?

    a. Matthew 18:11

    b. John 12:47, 48

    c. 1 Timothy 2:5, 6

    d. 1 John 4:14

6. What specific lessons did you learn today? *(Truths to depend on; promises to believe; warnings to heed; examples to follow.)*

7. Write these lessons in the form of a question to yourself. *(What should I do? What should I not be doing? Do I truly believe these truths?)*

DAY 5—BEGIN IN PRAYER

1. Read John 3:1–21.

2. Re-read John 3:19–21.

3. Today we study the ultimate contrast—light and darkness. Light expels darkness and exposes all that seeks to hide in darkness. What do we learn about the light?

   a. Psalm 27:1

   b. Isaiah 60:20

   c. John 12:46

   d. 1John 1:5

   e. Matthew 5:14–16

4. Now, compare what the Scriptures tell us about darkness.

   a. Matthew 22:13

   b. John 12:35b

   c. Ephesians 6:12

d. Colossians 1:13

e. 1 John 2:9–11

5. As *"children of the light,"* it is our responsibility to lead others from darkness to light. Find two Scriptures under each of the following topics that you could use to point the lost to the light.

a. Everyone needs a Savior

1.

2.

b. Salvation is a gift from God

1.

2.

c. Salvation comes by repentance and confession

1.

2.

d. You can have assurance that you are saved

1.

2.

6. What specific lessons did you learn today? *(Truths to depend on; promises to believe; warnings to heed; examples to follow.)*

7. Write these lessons in the form of a question to yourself. *(What should I do? What should I not be doing? Do I truly believe these truths?)*

DAY 6—BEGIN IN PRAYER

1. Read John 3:1–21.

2 What specific areas has the Lord spoken to you about this week? Are you positive of your citizenship in the Kingdom of God? Nicodemus came by night, are you willing to let everyone know about your love for the Lord? Are you able to tell others specific directions to the light?

3. Complete your memory verse today.

For God so loved the world, that He gave His only begotten Son, that whosoever believeth in Him should not perish, but have everlasting life. John 3:16

DAY 1—BEGIN IN PRAYER

1. Read John 3:22–36.

2. This section begins with an abrupt change of scene where two groups were baptizing: John the Baptist with his disciples, Jesus with his disciples. What attitude do you detect in the words of each of the following men? Record their words that exhibit this heart attitude.

   John the Baptist:

   John's Disciples:

3. Where do we get the gifts and the abilities to serve the Lord? (Record reference.) Do we ever have any excuse for pride? Who *must* receive the glory?

4. Choose a verse to memorize this week. *Begin working on it now.*

DAY 2—BEGIN IN PRAYER

1. Read John 3:22–36.

2. Re-read John 3:22–24.

3. Jesus and His disciples had left Jerusalem and traveled out of the city. John was much further north in Aenon near Salim. Use a Bible Map and locate Judea and Salim (in Samaria). Notice the distance between the two locations. Why may there have been *much water* there?

4. Often we worry, trying to be positive about what the Lord would have us to do and where we ought to do it. Here we learn a good lesson seeing that John the Baptist was instructed by God to point the way to Jesus and prepare those who chose to follow Jesus by baptizing them in water. Why had John the Baptist chosen this place?

   What are we to do to discover the will of God?

   a. Psalm 25:9, 10

   b. Psalm 37:4, 5

   c. Proverbs 3:5, 6

   d. Proverbs 16:3

   e. John 15:7

5. This baptism that John and Jesus' disciples practiced was different from what we as believers practice today. John's baptism was in preparation for salvation that was soon to come through the death and resurrection of Jesus. Today, we are baptized as a symbol of our commitment to Jesus as our Lord and Savior. What do we learn about water baptism in the following verses? Is baptism necessary for salvation?

a. Acts 8:26–39

b. 1Corinthians 1:13–18

c. Romans 10:9, 10

d. Mark 16:16 *(What is the reason for a person being damned?)*

e. Romans 6:1–6

6. What specific lessons did you learn today? *(Truths to depend on; promises to believe; warnings to heed; examples to follow.)*

7. Write these lessons in the form of a question to yourself. *(What should I do? What should I not be doing? Do I truly believe these truths?)*

DAY 3—BEGIN IN PRAYER

1. Read John 3:22–36.

2. Re-read John 3:25–29.

3. There was a question (or discussion, or debate) between the disciples of John and the Jews. It may have begun regarding "purification" but had become a competition for John's disciples. "All men come to him" was their complaint. As believers, we are to be keenly aware that it is God's work we do, for God's glory, by God's strength and as God leads. What reminders do we receive about competition in ministry?

   a. Romans 12:15, 16

   b. 1Corinthians 12:25, 26

   c. Hebrews 13:3

   d. 1Peter 3:8–12

4. John's reply, *"A man can receive nothing except it be given him from heaven,"* is echoed throughout the Scriptures. What more can we learn about this truth?

   a. Romans 12:5–8

   b. 1Corinthians 2:12–14

c. 1 Corinthians 4:7

d. 1 Corinthains 15:10

5. John employed a beautiful metaphor to depict the way he saw his relationship with Jesus the Christ. He described himself as the bridegroom's friend or the "best man." As the best man, John enjoyed seeing his friend, the bridegroom, honored. He insisted that all the attention go to the Lord and this caused his joy to be fulfilled. When we serve the Lord, we must be sure that all the attention *and glory* belongs to the Lord and in doing this we will experience fullness of joy. Study the following verses about our joy that comes from faithfully pointing the way to the Savior Jesus Christ.

a. Psalm 16:11

b. Proverbs 11:30

c. Matthew 25:21

d. John 17:13–19

6. What specific lessons did you learn today? *(Truths to depend on; promises to believe; warnings to heed; examples to follow.)*

7. Write these lessons in the form of a question to yourself. *(What should I do? What should I not be doing? Do I truly believe these truths?)*

DAY 4—BEGIN IN PRAYER *(Don't forget Who the Teacher is.)*

1. Read John 3:22–36.

2. Re-read John 3:30–33.

3. The word *"must"* is used three different times in this chapter. What truths *"must"* we believe and obey?

   a. John 3:7 — The "must" of a sinner -

   b. John 3:14 — The "must" of a Savior -

   c. John 3:30 — The "must" of a servant -

4. John, speaking of Jesus, tells us: *"He that comes from above is above all. And what He has seen and heard, He testifieth."* What do we learn from the following verses about Jesus' testimony?

   a. John 5:20–23

   b. John 7:16–18

c. John 8:26

d. John 15:15

5. The Lord's teachings are not to be studied intellectually, separated from everyday life. They are to be learned and obeyed. What is the test of true faith?

a. Matthew 7:21–24

b. John 14:23, 24

c. James 1:25

d. Revelation 22:14

6. What specific lessons did you learn today? *(Truths to depend on; promises to believe; warnings to heed; examples to follow.)*

7. Write these lessons in the form of a question to yourself. *(What should I do? What should I not be doing? Do I truly believe these truths?)*

DAY 5—BEGIN IN PRAYER

1. Read John 3:22–36.

2. Re-read John 3:34–36.

3. The Spirit of God, even in inspired prophets, was but a partial and intermittent gift; but in Jesus, the Son of God, the Spirit of God dwelt fully and uninterruptedly. Jesus was, and is, fully God and fully man, yet while He lived on earth He was dependent on the power and the work of the Holy Spirit in His ministry. Research this truth through the following Scriptures.

    a. Isaiah 11:1–5

    b. Isaiah 42:1–4

    c. Matthew 3:16, 17

    d. Acts 10:37, 38

4. What is the work of the Holy Spirit in our lives, as believers?

    a. Ezekiel 36:27

b. John 16:13–15

c. Acts 1:8

d. Romans 8:16

5. In verse 36 we have an eternal promise and an eternal warning. Believe on the Son—**life**; believe not the Son—**wrath**. There is no element of hoping—no maybe—no room for another way. In believing on the Son, everlasting life is assured—refusing to believe brings everlasting judgment. Allow the Lord to make this truth part of your life and heart by spending time meditating on the following Scriptures. *(Don't hurry through!)*

a. John 5:24

b. John 10:27–29

c. John 14:6

d. Romans 5:8–10

e. 1 Thessalonians 5:9

6. What specific lessons did you learn today? *(Truths to depend on; promises to believe; warnings to heed; examples to follow.)*

7. Write these lessons in the form of a question to yourself. *(What should I do? What should I not be doing? Do I truly believe these truths?)*

DAY 6—BEGIN IN PRAYER

1. Read John 3:22–36.

2. What specific lessons has the Lord taught you this week? Are you making every effort to make any necessary changes? Are you careful to give all the glory to God when He uses you? Is there jealousy or competition in your heart? Are you willing to *"decrease"* so that the Lord can *"increase"*? Are you confident in the assurance of your salvation?

    Spend some time in prayer over these lessons. Allow the Lord to speak to your heart.

3. Have you completed your memory verse? *Finish it today.*

We must never forget the cost of the blessings we have received through the Lord Jesus Christ. For us to be born into the family, Jesus Christ had to die. For us to enter into the loving relationship of salvation, He had to endure the hatred and condemnation of men. He had to be lifted up on the cross so that we might experience forgiveness and eternal life. May we never take this for granted.
—Warren Wiersbe

He must increase, but I must decrease. John 3:30

DAY 1—BEGIN IN PRAYER

1. Read John 4:1–30.

   Jesus had to go through Samaria not because of geography but because of His mission. Jews avoided Samaria because there was a long-standing, deep-seated hatred between them and the Samaritans. The Samaritans were a mixed race, part Jew and part Gentile, that grew out of the Assyrian captivity of the ten northern tribes in 727 B.C.

2. Re-read John 4:1–30.

   How do you think that Jesus feels about the Samaritans? (Give references from the Bible account to prove your point.)

   What does Jesus reveal about Himself?

   a. Verse 10

   b. Verses 25–26

3. How does the woman at the well address Jesus in each of the following verses?

   a. Verse 9

   b. Verse 11

Jesus
CHRIST—
son of GOD

c. Verse 19

d. Verse 29

4.   Chose a verse to memorize this week. *Begin working on it now.*

DAY 2—BEGIN IN PRAYER

1.   Read John 4:1–30.

2.   Re-read John 4:1–9.

3.   Jesus and His disciples leave Judea and start back toward Galilee choosing to pass through Samaria. Just as Jesus had spoken to Nicodemus regarding eternal life, here He chooses to reveal this truth to a woman. Jesus breaks some longstanding prejudices as He speaks to this Samaritan woman. He reveals His heart and gives us an example to follow when reaching out to the lost. Read the following Scriptures that further reveal our Lord's compassion for the lost and outcast of the world.

a. Luke 5:30–32

b. Luke 7:37–39, 47-50

c. Luke 19:7–10

d. Romans 5:8

4.   To whom are we to take the Gospel? How?

a. Psalm 96:1–4

b. Matthew 9:13

c. Mark 16:15

d. Luke 24:46–48

5.   This woman came to the well at an unusual hour (noon). Women usually drew water later in the day when it was cooler. Do you think that this is a significant fact? If so, why?

6.   What specific lessons did you learn today? *(Truths to depend on; promises to believe; warnings to heed; examples to follow.)*

7. Write these lessons in the form of a question to yourself. *(What should I do? What should I not be doing? Do I truly believe these truths?)*

DAY 3—BEGIN IN PRAYER

1. Read John 4:1–30.

2. Re-read John 4:10–19. (It will only take an extra 2 minutes.)

3. This woman of Samaria was dissatisfied, unfulfilled, and in need of the answer to her hopeless life. *Have you experienced her despair? Do you know others like her?* She came face to face with the answer to her emptiness, she needed the *"gift of God."* What more can we learn about the *"gift of God"* from the following verses?

    a. Romans 5:13–17

    b. Romans 6:23

    c. 2Corinthians 9:15

    d. Ephesians 2:8

4. Jesus spoke to this woman, and to us, regarding the need for *"living water."* In the Old Testament many verses speak of thirsting after God. In promising to give *"living water"* that would quench our thirst for God, Jesus was saying that He was the Messiah. Research these references in the Old Testament that point to Jesus.

a. Psalm 36:8–9

b. Isaiah 55:1

c. Jeremiah 2:13

d. Jeremiah 17:13

5. Mankind is in need of water daily because his thirst will return. The Samaritan woman needed to return every day for water. Likewise spiritually, the world and sometimes even Christians, try to satisfy this thirst with things that continually result in emptiness. When we try to fill this need with anything (love, sex, material things, power, pleasure, food, drugs), the end result is emptiness and despair. What encouragement do we receive from the following verses concerning God's sufficiency in our lives?

a. Psalm 27:1

b. Psalm 62:1, 2

c. Colossians 2:9, 10

d. Colossians 3:1–3

6. What specific lessons did you learn today? *(Truths to depend on; promises to believe; warnings to heed; examples to follow.)*

7. Write these lessons in the form of a question to yourself. *(What should I do? What should I not be doing? Do I truly believe these truths?)*

DAY 4—BEGIN IN PRAYER

1. Read John 4:1–30.

2. Re-read John 4:20–26.

3. One of the main points of contention between the Jews and the Samaritans was where was the proper place to worship God. The Jews worshipped in Jerusalem, the Samaritan on Mt. Gerizim. The woman wanted to know what the *prophet* thought to be true. He told her of a worship that neither of the groups knew, *"worship in spirit and in truth."* What can we learn about worship from the Psalms?

    a. Psalm 29:2

    b. Psalm 81:8–11

    c. Psalm 95:6, 7

d. Psalm 99:9

e. Psalm 138:2

4. When Jesus taught that worship must be *"in spirit,"* He was emphasizing the proper relationship with God. We approach Him on His terms, not ours. But His terms are for our benefit. We are to worship in submission to what God has revealed about Himself. Worship includes our praise, our confession, our thanksgiving, our request to draw closer to Him. God must be at the center of true spiritual worship. What reasons are given in the following verses that cause us to worship Him?

a. Jeremiah 31:3

b. John 1:12

c. Romans 8:17

d. Ephesians 2:1–5

e. Philippians 4:19

f. Colossians 1:16–19

5. This woman at the well knew that Messiah would someday come and answer all their questions, but to her surprise she was face to face with the *"I AM."* Use the following Scriptures to trace this description of God through the Bible.

a. Exodus 3:14

b. Isaiah 44:6

c. Isaiah 48:12

d. John 8:58

e. Revelation 1:8

f. Revelation 1:17, 18

6. What specific lessons did you learn today? *(Truths to depend on; promises to believe; warnings to heed; examples to follow.)*

7. Write these lessons in the form of a question to yourself. *(What should I do? What should I not be doing? Do I truly believe these truths?)*

DAY 5—BEGIN IN PRAYER

1. Read John 4:1–30.

2. Re-read 4:27–30.

3. *Personal:* The disciples *"marveled"* that He spoke to this woman. They obviously were not free from the prejudice that was so prevalent at the time. *How do you perceive those whose lifestyle doesn't line up with your standards? Are you willing to reach out to the lost and rejected with the answer to eternal, abundant life?*

4. Leaving her water jar, the woman went back to town. We can guess that she intended to return for it but she had to tell everyone whom she had met. Notice this fourth description of Jesus, *"Is not this the Christ?"* She could not wait to tell others and we ought to have this same zeal. What reminders do we receive from these verses regarding the necessity to redeem the time?

    a. Acts 13:47

    b. Romans 13:11–14

    c. Ephesians 5:14–17

d. Hebrews 12:1, 2

5. In summary, the woman was saying that Jesus could have told her everything about her life. This encounter with Jesus so touched her that she was willing to reveal her life. There is a change that takes place within the heart of the one who truly meets Jesus. They see their sin for what it is and are willing to leave it behind, this is repentance. Study 2 Corinthians 7:8–10 and record the difference between sorrow and repentance.

6. What specific lessons did you learn today? *(Truths to depend on; promises to believe; warnings to heed; examples to follow.)*

7. Write these lessons in the form of a question to yourself. *(What should I do? What should I not be doing? Do I truly believe these truths?)*

DAY 6—BEGIN IN PRAYER

1.   Read John 4:1–30.

2.   What specific lessons has the Lord taught you this week? Are you willing to take a less popular route for the sake of others? Have you accepted the gift of God—living water, everlasting life? Is your life characterized by the fountains of living water overflowing or are you still seeking other things to fulfill your life? Do you realize that He knows everything you have ever done? Is the worship in your life true worship — in spirit and truth? The answer is in verse 26—Jesus.

3.   Have you completed your memory verse this week. *Finish it now.*

God is a Spirit: and they that worship Him must worship Him in spirit and in truth. John 4:24

Jesus saith unto her, I that speak unto thee am He. John 4:26

DAY 1—BEGIN IN PRAYER

1. Read John 4:31–42.

2. Re-read John 4:31–42. What was the main concern of the following people?

    a. The disciples (vs. 31–33)

    b. Jesus (v. 34)

    c. Samaritans (v. 40)

3. Meditate on John 4:34. How true is this of you?

4. Choose a verse to memorize this week. *Begin working on it now.*

DAY 2—BEGIN IN PRAYER

1. Read John 4:31–42.

2. Re-read John 4: 31–34.

3. The use of the term *meat* gives us a picture of the importance of what Jesus was teaching the disciples (and us). We must have physical food if we are going to survive and flourish and even more importantly, as Christians, we need spiritual food to stay healthy and grow strong. What more do we learn about this analogy from the following verses?

    a. Job 23:12

b. Psalm 119:103

c. Jeremiah 15:16

d. 1 Peter 2:2

4. Take note of the response of the disciples. How is it similar to:

a. Nathanael (John 1:46)

b. The Jews at the Temple (John 2:18–21)

c. Nicodemus (John 3:4)

d. Samaritan woman (John 4:15)

5. We learn a valuable truth from verse 34, that is, in *doing the will of the Lord* we will find fulfillment. We will not find fulfillment from things, power, pleasure, relationships, or from daily food. We will only be fulfilled when we do the *will of the Father*. When we submit our life to the Father and willingly carry out His plan for our lives we will find true fulfillment and ultimate satisfaction. Record what you learn from the following verses.

a. Psalm 17:15

b. Psalm 107:8, 9

c. Matthew 5:6

d. Matthew 6:31–33

6.   What specific lessons did you learn today? *(Truths to depend on; promises to believe; warnings to heed; examples to follow.)*

7.   Write these lessons in the form of a question to yourself. *(What should I do? What should I not be doing? Do I truly believe these truths?)*

DAY 3—BEGIN IN PRAYER

1.   Read John 4:31–42.

2,   Re-read John 35–38.

3.   The lesson to learn today is that we desperately need spiritual perception. When we view the world through our physical eyes and with our natural perception, we can only get a vision that is according to the world system. Jesus tells us, *"don't say four months, and then the harvest,"* because this is not the truth in the spiritual realm. (It may have been that this was a common term used by the farmers because this is the approximate time between planting and

harvesting.) Instead He tells us, *"the fields are white already to harvest."* What do we learn about this spiritual harvest from Matthew 9:37, 38?

a. Description of the harvest:

b. Number of laborers:

c. Way to increase laborers:

d. Whose harvest is it?

e. Who sends forth the laborers?

4. Look up the definition of the following words for a better understanding of our calling:

a. Harvest (John 4:35)

b. Sows (John 4:36, 37)

c. Reaps (John 4:38)

d. Labor (v. 38)

5.   As believers we are **all called** to participate in this sowing and reaping process. It is a joint venture and neither part is more or less important. Often we reap where we have not sown, when someone prays with us to enter into the Kingdom of God, because someone has gone before us in prayer and witnessing. Also, we can be encouraged when we witness with seemingly no results that this is the work of the sower. What warnings and encouragements do we find for our labor?

a. Matthew 10:16–20

b. Luke 10:3

c. Galatians 6:7–9

d. James 5:7, 8

6.   What specific lessons did you learn today? *(Truths to depend on; promises to believe; warnings to heed; examples to follow.)*

7. Write these lessons in the form of a question to yourself. *(What should I do? What should I not be doing? Do I truly believe these truths?)*

DAY 4—BEGIN IN PRAYER *(Call on the Lord.)*

1. Read John 4:31–42.

2. Re-read John 4:39, 40.

3. The disciples may have complained in their hearts, "why are we wasting time with the Samaritans anyway, they don't use the whole Bible or worship in Jerusalem as the Jews." But look at the results of the discussion with this woman in verse 39. Many believed. How often do we think that it may be hopeless to share? Record the promises and encouragement we receive from the following verses.

    a. Isaiah 55:11

    b. Romans 1:16

    c. Romans 10:17

    d. Hebrews 4:12

4. The Lord knows the heart and the actions of every man and woman, which means that He knows *your* heart and *your* actions. What does He find when He searches your heart? What ought He find?

    a. Psalm 24:3–5

    b. 2Corinthians 7:1

    c. Hebrews 10:22–25

    d. James 4:8–10

5. When the Samaritans came to Jesus, they desired that He would come and stay with them so that they could know Him personally and learn from Him. This is a great example for us to follow. As Christians, it is absolutely necessary that we have intimate fellowship with the Lord through daily Bible Study and Prayer. What do we learn from the following examples that we can apply to our lives?

    a. Proverbs 8:34

    b. Luke 10:39; 41

    c. Luke 21:37, 38

d. John 8:2

6. What specific lessons did you learn today? *(Truths to depend on; promises to believe; warnings to heed; examples to follow.)*

7. Write these lessons in the form of a question to yourself. *(What should I do? What should I not be doing? Do I truly believe these truths?)*

DAY 5—BEGIN IN PRAYER

1. Read John 4:31–42. *(Don't quit now!)*

2. Re-read John 4:41–42.

3. Record the reaction of those who heard Jesus speak?

    a. Matthew 7:28, 29

    b. Luke 4:32

    c. John 7:46

4. Jesus stayed with them for two days and because He did, many more believed because of His *Word*. What can we learn about the power of God's *Word* to bring salvation?

a. Psalm 119:50

b. John 6:63

c. 1 Thessalonians 2:13

d. 1 Peter 1:23

5. The belief of the people caused them to declare, *"this is indeed the Christ, the Savior of the world."* What encouragement do you receive from the following examples to declare this truth to those who don't believe?

a. Acts 4:1–4

b. Acts 8:35–38

c. Acts 18:24–28

d. 1Corinthians 2:1–5

6.   What specific lessons did you learn today? *(Truths to depend on; promises to believe; warnings to heed; examples to follow.)*

7.   Write these lessons in the form of a question to yourself. *(What should I do? What should I not be doing? Do I truly believe these truths?)*

DAY 6—BEGIN IN PRAYER

1.   Read John 1:31–42.

2.   What specific lessons has the Lord taught you this week? What is it that brings satisfaction in your life? Do you find your fulfillment in doing the will of the Father? Do you see the harvest as *white,* or do you sometimes delay—thinking—*there is still four months?* Do you see the necessity (and joy) of sowing even though reaping seems more profitable? Are you daily asking the Lord to abide with you? Do you recognize the power of the Word of God for salvation? Are you actively telling others about the Christ, the Savior of the world?

Allow the Lord to make any of these changes, He is waiting to use you mightily to reach a lost and dying world.

Jesus saith unto them, My meat is to do the will of Him that sent Me, and to finish His work. John 4:34

DAY 1—BEGIN IN PRAYER

1. Read John 4:43–54.

2. Re-read John 4:43–54. What was the reason for each of the following to be seeking Jesus?

   a. The Galileans (v. 45)

   b. The Nobleman (vs. 47; 49)

3. *"Wonders,"* in verse 48, suggests the purely miraculous and amazing. The people were interested in the spectacular, but not in signs that pointed to God and demanded a response of faith and allegiance. Did faith based on miracles satisfy Jesus?

   a. John 2:23, 24

   b. John 4:48

   c. John 20:29

4. What is mature faith based on? See Hebrews 11:6.

5. Choose a verse to memorize this week. *Begin working on it now.*

DAY 2—BEGIN IN PRAYER

1. Read John 4:43–54.

2. Re-read John 4:43–45.

3. Jesus and the disciples left Samaria and went again into Galilee even though He knew that He would not be accepted there. He went to the Galileans knowing that they would welcome Him as a miracle-worker but not as a prophet, much less as the Messiah.

   Have you ever experienced this feeling from those who are closest to you when you try to tell them about the Lord? What can we learn from the following verses to encourage us to be faithful to go to them?

   a. Matthew 10:22

   b. Luke 6:22, 23

   c. John 15:18–20

   d. John 17:14–16

4. Jesus was faithful to go to those who are described in Matthew 4 as *"those who sat in darkness."* Have you ever been afraid to share the Gospel with those who "sit in darkness"? How can we overcome this fear?

   a. 1John 1:9

b. Acts 1:8

c. Acts 4:13

d. Acts 4:29–31

5. The Galileans welcomed Jesus because they had seen the miracles that He had done at the Feast. Many people seek Jesus *for what He can do* for them instead of *for Who He is*. What does the Bible say about Who He is?

   a. Colossians 1:16

   b. Hebrews 1:1, 2

   c. 1Peter 1:18, 19

   d. Revelation 5:12

6. What specific lessons did you learn today? *(Truths to depend on; promises to believe; warnings to heed; examples to follow.)*

7. Write these lessons in the form of a question to yourself. *(What should I do? What should I not be doing? Do I truly believe these truths?)*

DAY 3—BEGIN IN PRAYER

1. Read John 4:43–54.

2. Re-read John 4:46–50.

3. Jesus came again into Cana where He had turned water into wine and He encounters a certain nobleman which means "kings man" so he may have been related to or a servant of royalty. He undoubtedly had heard that Jesus could work miracles so he made his request of the Lord. When we truly seek the Lord, He meets us right where we are at, even with an imperfect faith as this nobleman had. What do we learn from the following verses about faith?

    a. Matthew 17:20

    b. Matthew 21:21

    c. Acts 3:12–16

    d. Romans 1:17

4. There is a similar account of a man who came to Jesus recorded in Matthew 8:5–13. Read the account comparing it with this nobleman's story.

    What is similar?

    What is different?

    What was Jesus' reaction?

    What was the end result?

5. In John 4, notice the growth in this man's faith through his discussion with Jesus that only lasted moments. Record what you find.

    What was the man's initial request? (vs. 47; 49)

    What did he do when Jesus spoke to him? (v. 50)

    What do we need to do to increase our faith in the Lord Jesus Christ?

    a. Psalm 19:7–10

    b. Hebrews 5:12–14

c. 1 Peter 2:2

d. 2 Peter 3:17, 18

6. What specific lessons did you learn today? *(Truths to depend on; promises to believe; warnings to heed; examples to follow.)*

7. Write these lessons in the form of a question to yourself. *(What should I do? What should I not be doing? Do I truly believe these truths?)*

DAY 4—BEGIN IN PRAYER *(Don't forget!)*

1. Read John 4: 43–54.

2. Re-read John 4:51–54.

3. The Lord Jesus is the Lord of time and space and He knows all things. The nobleman inquired as to the time that his son was healed and it was the same hour that Jesus said unto him *"thy son liveth."* Jesus is the healer of our soul, our mind, our heart, and our body. What more can you learn from the following Scriptures?

a. Exodus 15:26

b. Psalms 103:1–5

c. Psalm 147:1–6

d. James 5:13–15

4. The outcome of faith is rest. The nobleman went away believing and the outcome of that belief is rest. *Are you resting in His Word as true and faithful?* What encouragement do you find from these verses?

a. Deuteronomy 7:9

b. Deuteronomy 32:3, 4

c. Matthew 11:28–30

d. 1Peter 4:19

5. Notice the effect of a strong belief on an entire household. Look up the following references and see the reoccurring truth.

a. Joshua 24:15

b. Acts 16:14, 15

c. Acts 18:8

d. 2Timothy 1:5

6. What specific lessons did you learn today? *(Truths to depend on; promises to believe; warnings to heed; examples to follow.)*

7. Write these lessons in the form of a question to yourself. *(What should I do? What should I not be doing? Do I truly believe these truths?)*

DAY 5—BEGIN IN PRAYER

1. Read John 4:43–53.

2. What specific lessons have you learned this week? Are you doing them? Why are *you* seeking Jesus? Do you trust that He is able to do whatever is best for you? Are you resting in that trust?

3. Read and write out Philippians 4:6, 7. Ask the Lord to help you put this promise into practice starting now. Write out a prayer to Him.

4. Have you completed your memory verse for this week? *Finish it today.*

DAY 6—BEGIN IN PRAYER

1. Read John 1–4. *(The whole thing, you can do it!)*

2. Review Day 6 of each of the studies (this is very important) with these questions in mind:

How have I grown spiritually?

What **specific** areas have changed?

What one **specific** area is most in need of surrender to the Lord?

Will you surrender it to Him today? Seek Him in prayer because only He can transform your life and He is longing to do so.

DAY 1—BEGIN IN PRAYER

1. Read the Gospel of John chapters 1–12. *(Slowly—thinking about what you read.)*

DAY 2—BEGIN IN PRAYER

1. Read the Gospel of John chapters 13–21. *(This is your Heavenly Father speaking to **you**.)*

Note: The Key Verse of the Gospel of John is John 20:31.

2. Memorize this verse. Begin working on it today.

DAY 3—BEGIN IN PRAYER

1. Read John 5–6.

2. Make a list of what Jesus declared about Himself and His mission (include chapter and reference).

Make a list of how the crowd or the disciples reacted to His declaration (include chapter and reference).

Make a list of how the Scribes and Pharisees reacted to His declaration (include chapter and reference).

3.   Give a Title to each of the chapters (a five to seven word description that would help remind you of it's contents).

Chapter 5:

Chapter 6:

DAY 4—BEGIN IN PRAYER

1.   Read John 7–8.

2.   Continue adding to your lists for chapters 7–8.

a. What did Jesus declare about Himself and His mission?

b. How did the crowd or the disciples react to His declaration?

c. How did the Scribes and Pharisees react to His declaration?

3.   Give a Title to each of the chapters.

Chapter 7:

Chapter 8:

DAY 5—BEGIN IN PRAYER

1. Read John 9–10.

2. Continue adding to your lists for chapters 9–10.

    a. What did Jesus declare about Himself and His mission?

    b. How did the crowd and the disciples react to His declaration?

    c. How did the Scribes and Pharisees react to His declaration?

3. Give a Title to each of the chapters.

    Chapter 9:

    Chapter 10:

DAY 6—BEGIN IN PRAYER

1. Read John 11–12.

2. Continue adding to your list for chapters 11–12.

a. What did Jesus declare about Himself and His mission?

b. How did the crowd and the disciples react to His declaration?

c. How did the Scribes and Pharisees react to His declaration?

3. Give a Title to each of the chapters.

Chapter 11:

Chapter 12:

*Close your study time in prayer asking the Lord to teach you through your diligent study of these upcoming lessons. Remember it is the Holy Spirit who teaches you and it is God's Word that changes your life. Allow the work to be done by surrendering your will to **His** daily. May the Lord richly bless you as you seek Him.*

All scripture is given by inspiration of God, and is profitable for doctrine, for reproof, for correction, for instruction in righteousness. 2 Timothy 3:16

DAY 1—BEGIN IN PRAYER

1. Read John 5:1–30.

2. Why do you think Jesus chose to heal the man on the Sabbath?

3. What effect did this miracle have on the heart and life of this man? (vs. 9; 14)

4. What effect did it have on the hearts of the Jews? (vs. 10; 16)

5. Choose a verse to memorize this week. Begin working on it now.

DAY 2—BEGIN IN PRAYER

1. Read John 5:1–30.

2. Re-read John 5:1–9.

3. Now Jesus had gone up to Jerusalem for a feast and came to a place where the hopeless, helpless and lost gathered. They were seeking healing and into their presence comes the Savior, the Healer, the Messiah. What more can we learn from the following verses?

    a. Isaiah 42:6, 7

    b. Isaiah 42:16

c. Isaiah 61:1–3

d. Luke 4:17–21

4.   Jesus asked this question, *"wilt thou be made whole?"* Today He asks the same question of every person. Jesus will not force Himself on anyone. We must recognize our need and seek Him and when we do the transformation is absolute. What do we learn about this transformation from the following verses?

a. Ezekiel 11:19, 20

b. Romans 6:4–6

c. Romans 8:9, 10

d. 2Corinthians 5:17

5.   The results of a face-to-face encounter with the Lord is transformation, but the proof of transformation is obedience. Jesus told the man: *"Rise, take up thy bed, and walk,"* and immediately he did so. What instructions do we find about obedience in the following verses?

a. 1Samuel 15:22

b. John 14:23, 24

c. John 15:10

d. Romans 6:16

6.   What specific lesson did you learn today? *(Truths to depend on; promises to believe; warnings to heed; examples to follow / not follow.)*

7.   Write these lessons in the form of a question to yourself. *(What should I do? What should I not be doing? Do I truly believe these truths? Do I need to make any changes?)*

DAY 3—BEGIN IN PRAYER

1.   Read John 5:1–30.

2.   Re-read John 5:10–16. *(No cheating!)*

3.   There is nothing in God's law to prohibit a person from carrying a mat on the Sabbath. Carrying a mat broke the Pharisees' legalistic application of God's command. They had created a long list of rules and regulations that turned Sabbath keeping into a chore and an impossible burden. What reaction did Jesus have to these Pharisees' legalistic rules?

a. Matthew 23:2–5

b. Matthew 23:13

c. Matthew 23:23

4.   What was the purpose of the Sabbath?

a. Exodus 20:8–11

b. Isaiah 58:13, 14

c. Mark 2:27, 28

d. Hebrews 4:1–10 *(Jesus is our "Sabbath" rest.)*

5.   The religious leaders had created a law that people could not heal on the Sabbath because healing was "work." Record a few details from each of the following accounts of Sabbath miracles with our Lord performed.

a. Mark 1:21–28

b. Mark 1:29–31

c. Mark 3:1–6

d. Luke 13:10–17

e. Luke 14:1–6

f. John 9:1–16

6. What specific lesson did you learn today? *(Truths to depend on; promises to believe; warnings to heed; examples to follow / not follow.)*

7. Write these lessons in the form of a question to yourself. *(What should I do? What should I not be doing? Do I truly believe these truths? Do I need to make any changes?)*

DAY 4—BEGIN IN PRAYER

1. Read John 5:1–30.

2. Re-read John 5:17–30. *(We will cover these verses in two days.)*

3. In this section of chapter 5 we are given the Lord's own teaching regarding the absolute equality of the Son with the Father. There is no mistaking the claim He was making—He was and is—God. Record the reaction of the Jews.

4. Record the declarations Jesus made about Himself, His works, and His relationship with the Father?

    a. Verses 17, 18

    b. Verse 19

    c. Verse 20

    d. Verse 21

    e. Verses 22, 23

    f. Verses 24–26

    g. Verses 27–30

5. The following verses give us a partial description of the work of God. Record what you learn.

    a. Psalm 7:6–11

    b. Psalm 9:7, 8

    c. Isaiah 35:3–7

d. Genesis 1:20–27

e. Deuteronomy 32:39

f. 1Samuel 2:6

6.   What specific lesson did you learn today? *(Truths to depend on; promises to believe; warnings to heed; examples to follow / not follow.)*

7.   Write these lessons in the form of a question to yourself. *(What should I do? What should I not be doing? Do I truly believe these truths? Do I need to make any changes?)*

DAY 5—BEGIN IN PRAYER

1.   Read John 5:1–30.

2.   Re-read John 5:17–30.

3.   Yesterday we recorded a list of the work of God. Today, record the facts and truths about the work of the Messiah (Savior).

a. Daniel 7:13, 14

b. Jeremiah 23:5, 6

c. Isaiah 53:4, 5

d. Isaiah 61:1–3

4. Now, compare these truths about the Messiah with Jesus' declaration and description of Himself by reviewing your answers on Day 4, Question #4.

    What evidence do you find of the Deity of Jesus Christ?

5. Re-read verse 24. *"Verily, verily"* means: *listen up, very important truth.* This is a promise that when you hear Jesus' words and believe you shall have (possess) eternal life.

    So then faith cometh by hearing, and hearing by the Word of God.
    Romans 10:17

    We need not doubt our salvation when we truly lay our lives in His hands and rely on His sacrifice for our salvation. What encouragements and comfort do we receive from these Scriptures?

    a. John 3:36a

b. John 6:40

c. Romans 8:16, 17

d. 1John 5:11–13

6.   What specific lesson did you learn today? *(Truths to depend on; promises to believe; warnings to heed; examples to follow / not follow.)*

7.   Write these lessons in the form of a question to yourself. *(What should I do? What should I not be doing? Do I truly believe these truths? Do I need to make any changes?)*

DAY 6—BEGIN IN PRAYER

1.   Read John 5:1–30.

2.   What specific lessons has the Lord spoken to you about this week? Are you among those seeking an answer other than Jesus? Do you see the multitudes of hopeless, helpless people seeking the answer and respond like the Pharisees? Is your heart tender toward those who need to know Jesus? Do your realize that Jesus is the only answer for your infirmities? Since Jesus has

made you *"whole,"* how are you doing in being obedient to His Word? Are you truly convinced that Jesus is God? Could you explain His Deity to others?

3. Spend some time in prayer truly asking the Lord to show you the areas He desires to change in your life. Will you allow Him to?

4. Have you completed your memory verse for this week? *Finish it today.*

Verily, verily, I say unto you, He that heareth My Word, and believeth on Him that sent Me, hath everlasting life, and shall not come into condemnation; but is passed from death unto life. John 5:24

DAY 1—BEGIN IN PRAYER

1. Read John 5:31–47.

2. A key word in this passage of Scripture would be *"witness."* What witnesses to His identity does Jesus name in the following verses?

    a. Verses 5:33–35

    b. Verse 5:36

    c. Verse 5:37

    d. Verse 5:39

    e. Verse 5:46

3. Look up the definition of the following words for a better understanding of their meaning. *(Use a Bible Dictionary, Vine's Dictionary of New Testament Words, Strong's Concordance, or if you do not have access to the above, use a regular English Language Dictionary.)*

    a. Witness (v. 31)

Jesus
CHRIST
son of GOD

b. Works (v. 36)

c. Abiding (v. 38)

d. Receive (v. 43)

e. Believed (v. 46)

4.   Choose a verse to memorize this week. Begin working on it now.

DAY 2—BEGIN IN PRAYER

1.   Read John 5:31–47.

2.   Re-read John 5:31, 32.

3.   In chapter 5 we are studying an awesome miracle that was performed by Jesus and the confrontation that took place because of the unbelief of those who saw this miracle. Jesus proclaimed His Deity in verses 16–30 and now begins to outline the proof of His proclamation. In verses 31 and 32, He tells us that He does not bear witness of Himself independently of the Father but because they are One, the Father also bears witness of Him. What more can we learn from the following verses about this witness of the Father?

a. John 8:17, 18

b. Matthew 3:17

c. Matthew 17:5

d. 2Peter 1:16–18

4.   According to Jewish Law, truth or validity had to be established by two or three witnesses. Even though He needed not man to testify of Him, it appears that He chose to offer this proof for the sake of those willing to hear. (See verse 34.) Record what insight you gain regarding the need for two or three witnesses from the following references.

a. Deuteronomy 19:15

b. Matthew 18:15, 16

c. 2Corinthians 13:1

d. 1Timothy 5:19, 20

5.   The witness of the Father is true because the character of the Father is truth and righteousness. What more can we learn about the character of God?

a. Exodus 34:5–7

b. Deuteronomy 32:3, 4

c. 1 John 5:20

d. Revelation 16:7

6.   What specific lessons did you learn today? *(Truths to depend on; promises to believe; warnings to heed; examples to follow / not follow.)*

7.   Write these lessons in the form of a question to yourself. *(What should I do? What should I not be doing? Do I truly believe these truths? Do I need to make any changes?)*

DAY 3—BEGIN IN PRAYER
   (Remember it is the Holy Spirit Who teaches you.)

1.   Read John 5:31–47.

2.   Re-read John 5:33–36.

3.   Jesus gives us two witnesses that bear witness to His Deity. The first is John the Baptist. What declarations did he make about Jesus?

a. John 1:7–9

b. John 1:22, 23

c. John 1:26, 27

d. John 1:32–36

4. John the Baptist was that burning and shining "lamp." It is not the lamp that gives light but it is merely the vessel the holds the oil that produces light. So are we, as believers, simply the vessel that is to carry the Light (Jesus) to the world in darkness. What can we learn about the Light and our responsibility as the "lamp"?

    a. John 8:12

    b. John 9:5

    c. John 12:46

    d. Matthew 5:14–16 (To the "lamp.")

5. The second witness that Jesus gives us as proof of His deity is His *"works."* What more can you find out about His works from John's Gospel. (This is called a *word* study.)

a. John 10:25, 37, 38

b. John 14:10, 11

c. John 15:24

d. John 17:4

6.   What specific lessons did you learn today? *(Truths to depend on; promises to believe; warnings to heed; examples to follow / not follow.)*

7.   Write these lessons in the form of a question to yourself. *(What should I do? What should I not be doing? Do I truly believe these truths? Do I need to make any changes?)*

DAY 4—BEGIN IN PRAYER

1.   Read John 5:31–47.

2.   Re-read John 5:37–40.

3. It is the Father and His Spirit that ultimately bear witness of our relationship with God. It is not an audible voice or a faith in things we can see that prove our salvation. What is the proof of our salvation?

    a. Romans 8:15, 16

    b. Ephesians 1:13

    c. 1 John 4:12, 13

    d. 1 John 5:10–12

4. What do we learn about the importance of the Word of God *abiding* in our hearts and lives?

    a. Deuteronomy 6:6–9

    b. Psalm 119:11

    c. John 15:7

    d. 1 John 2:14

5. In verse 39 Jesus tells these *"religious"* men, *"ye search the Scriptures"* for eternal life. The Scriptures are full of testimony about the coming Messiah, yet they turned away from Him, *"Who is the Way, the Truth, and the Life."* *Are you searching? Do you know someone who is?* Jesus says the Scriptures themselves testify that He is the Messiah. Look up a **few** of the following prophecies and their fulfillment to encourage and strengthen your faith and witness.

Prophecy	Fulfillment
1. Micah 5:2	1. Matthew 2:1
2. Isaiah 7:14	2. Matthew 1:21–23
3. Isaiah 53:3	3. John 1:11
4. Psalm 22:16	4. John 19:23; John 20:27
5. Zechariah 12:10	5. John 19:34
6. Psalm 16:10	6. Matthew 28:6

Note: This is only a partial list of the prophecies fulfilled by Jesus regarding the Messiah.

6. What specific lessons did you learn today? *(Truths to depend on; promises to believe; warnings to heed; examples to follow / not follow.)*

7. Write these lessons in the form of a question to yourself. *(What should I do? What should I not be doing? Do I truly believe these truths? Do I need to make any changes?)*

DAY 5—BEGIN IN PRAYER

1. Read John 5:31–47.

2. Re-read John 5:41–47.

3. Jesus knew their hearts and that their love was not from God nor toward Him. What do we learn about God's love and the effect that it *must* have on our lives and actions?

    a. Luke 16:15

    b. John 8:47

    c. 1John 2:15

    d. 1John 4:20, 21

4. The words of condemnation in verse 44 expose why these Jewish religious leaders would not believe. They were more interested in the praise and approval of men then they were in obtaining the praise of God.

What do the following Scriptures teach regarding "the praise of man"?

a. Matthew 6:1–6

b. Matthew 23:5–7

c. John 12:42, 43

d. Acts 4:18–20

5. Jesus ended this discussion with a warning to these Jewish leaders that Moses, whom they honored, would be their judge. The very Scriptures (written by Moses) they used to defend their religion would one day bear witness against their unbelief. They professed to believe Moses but they didn't believe what he wrote. In like manner, we often claim to believe in Jesus but refuse to believe and be obedient to God's Word. What exhortation and warning do we find in these verses?

a. Ezekiel 33:31, 32

b. Matthew 7:21–27

c. Luke 6:46

d. James 1:23–25

6.   What specific lessons did you learn today? *(Truths to depend on; promises to believe; warnings to heed; examples to follow / not follow.)*

7.   Write these lessons in the form of a question to yourself. *(What should I do? What should I not be doing? Do I truly believe these truths? Do I need to make any changes?).*

DAY 6—BEGIN IN PRAYER

1.   Read John 5:31–47.

2.   What specific lessons has the Lord spoken to you about this week? Are you willing to allow Him to change these areas?

3.   *How confident are you in the faithfulness of the Father? John was a "burning and shining lamp." Are you? Is there outward evidence of your salvation in your life? Is God's Word abiding in your heart? Do you desire "the praise of men" more than the praise of God?*

Spend some time in prayer over the answers to these questions. It is the Lord who changes your heart—surrender it to His will.

4.   Have you completed your memory verse for this week? *Finish it today.*

Search the scriptures; for in them ye think ye have eternal life: and they are they which testify of Me. John 5:39

DAY 1—BEGIN IN PRAYER

1. Read John 6:1–21.

2. Re-read John 6:1–21 and record the two miracles, or "signs" that Jesus does to reveal His deity.

   a.

   b.

3. Read the account of this miracle in the other three Gospels and record any details not given to us by John.

   a. Matthew 14:13–33

   b. Mark 6:34–52

   c. Luke 9:12–17

4. Chose a verse to memorize this week. Begin working on it now.

DAY 2 —BEGIN IN PRAYER

1. Read John 6:1–21.

2. Re-read John 6:1–4.

Jesus
CHRIST
son of **GOD**

3.   John uses the expression of the time, *"after these things,"* to convey to us that some time has passed. In researching the timeline from a harmony of the Gospels we find that about one full year has passed. Many exciting and tragic events have occurred. Look up the following references and record the events leading up to the feeding of the 5,000. (Do not try to give details, only what events occurred.)

     a. Matthew 5–7

     b. Matthew 8:5–13

     c. Luke 7:11–17

     d. Mark 4:35–41

4.   Continue recording the events that occurred in Jesus' ministry prior to these miracles in Chapter 6.

     a. Mark 5:1–20

     b. Luke 8:40–56

     c. Matthew 10:1–16

d. Matthew 14:1–12

5.   Jesus and His disciples had crossed over the Sea of Galilee in order to escape the crowds for a time of private fellowship and teaching. However, the people sought Jesus because of the miracles that He did and they followed Him around the Lake. Though we do not find it easy to remove ourselves from the pressure of "things and needs" that crowd our lives, we find here that the Lord gives us a perfect example to follow regarding rest and fellowship with the Father. What encouragement do you receive from the following Scriptures?

a. Matthew 14:23

b. Mark 1:35

c. Luke 6:12

d. Luke 9:28

*Personal: Do you **daily** seek the Lord to surrender your will and your plans to His service and use?*

6.   What specific lessons did you learn today? *(Truths to depend on; promises to believe; warnings to heed; examples to follow / not to follow.)*

7. Write these lessons in the form of a question to yourself. *(What should I do? What should I not be doing? Do I truly believe these truths? Do I need to make any changes?)*

DAY 3—BEGIN IN PRAYER *(Don't Forget!)*

1. Read John 6:1–21.

2. Re-read John 6:5–9.

3. This great multitude of people presented an opportunity for the testing of the disciples faith. How were all of these people going to be fed? What do we learn from the following verses regarding the trials and testing of our faith?

   a. Deuteronomy 8:2, 3

   b. Romans 5:3–5

   c. James 1:2–4

   d. James 1:12

4. In usual use, the word test *(periazo)* has a neutral meaning. It refers to a proving experience. God allows testing in our lives not expecting failure but placing us in a position where our faith may grow stronger. What truths do we gain from these following tests?

    a. Genesis 22:1–12

    b. Matthew 4:1–11

5.   Impossible is not a word that is in God's vocabulary and yet often, like Phillip and Andrew, we are very short-sighted not believing there is an answer or a solution to the hardest things we face in life. Research the following verses and record what lessons and encouragement you receive.

    a. Genesis 18:13, 14

    b. Jeremiah 32:27

    c. Matthew 6:25, 26

    d. Matthew 19:26

    e. Philippians 4:19

6. What specific lessons did you learn today? *(Truths to depend on; promises to believe; warnings to heed; examples to follow / not to follow.)*

7. Write these lessons in the form of a question to yourself. *(What should I do? What should I not be doing? Do I truly believe these truths? Do I need to make any changes?)*

DAY 4—BEGIN IN PRAYER

1. Read John 6:1–21. *(It will become a part of your life.)*

2. Re-read John 6:10–15.

3. Jesus knew what He was going to do, therefore, He told the disciples to have the men sit down and they numbered 5000 men, plus women and children (Matthew 14:21). Jesus demonstrates for us the importance of knowing where our every meal comes from and accepting with a heart of thanksgiving. What do we learn about thanksgiving and thankfulness?

    a. Psalm 107:22

    b. Hebrews 13:15

    c. Philippians 4:6, 7

d. Ephesians 5:20

4. We can learn a lesson from the leftovers of this account. God gives in abundance. He takes whatever we offer him in time, ability, or resources and multiplies its effectiveness more than we might ever have imagined. He asks us to simply make ourselves available and He will do His work through us. What attitude do we find in these men and women who God used mightily?

    a. Jeremiah (Jeremiah 1:4–10)

    b. Isaiah (Isaiah 6:5–8)

    c. Mary (Luke 1:38)

    d. Paul (Acts 22:8–16)

5. When they saw the miracle that Jesus did, they proclaimed, *"this is of a truth the prophet (Deuteronomy 18:15–18) that is come unto the world."* The Jews were looking for a political king not a spiritual king. Some come to Jesus for what they can gain, yet the only right motive for coming to the Lord is because of Who He is. What do we learn from the following verses about Who God is and all that He has done for us?

    a. John 3:16, 17

    b. Hebrews 1:1–3

c. 1 Peter 1:18, 19

d. Revelation 1:5

6. What specific lessons did you learn today? *(Truths to depend on; promises to believe; warnings to heed; examples to follow / not to follow.)*

7. Write these lessons in the form of a question to yourself. *(What should I do? What should I not be doing? Do I truly believe these truths? Do I need to make any changes?)*

DAY 5—BEGIN IN PRAYER

1. Read John 6:1–21.

2. Re-read John 6:16–21 and read Matthew 14:25–32.

3. The disciples went down to the sea and entered into a ship and a storm arose by reason of a great wind. They had just witnessed the miracle of the multiplication of the loaves and fish and now they were facing a *storm (trial or test)*. Often, after an important spiritual lesson the enemy comes with a test. What are we to do when we face the storms of life?

a. 1 Chronicles 16:11

b. Matthew 4:1–11

c. Romans 8:28

d. James 4:7, 8

4. We are often plagued by fear and doubt and these are the result of not truly trusting the Lord with our very life, future and needs. What does the Bible say about fear and it's companions—doubt and worry?

a. Psalms 27:1–5

b. Isaiah 12:1–6

c. Matthew 6:25–34

d. Philippians 4:6, 7

e. 2Timothy 1:7

5.   *Personal: What do you most fear?*

What do you most worry about?

What is the worst that could happen?

Review the Scriptures from question #4 and spend time in prayer handing these fears over to the One who calms the storms and allows us to safely pass above them when our eyes are focused on Him. (Remember Peter began to sink when He looked at the storm.)

6.   What specific lessons did you learn today? *(Truths to depend on; promises to believe; warnings to heed; examples to follow/ not to follow.)*

7.   Write these lessons in the form of a question to yourself. *(What should I do? What should I not be doing? Do I truly believe these truths? Do I need to make any changes?)*

DAY 6—BEGIN IN PRAYER

1. Read John 6:1–21.

2. What specific lessons have you learned from the Lord this week? *Do you allow the pressure of people and things to crowd out your daily fellowship with the Lord? How do you respond to "seemingly" impossible circumstances? Do you have a thankful heart? How often do you find yourself complaining or whining? Is fear a part of your life? Do you realize that worry is a sin?*

    Allow the Lord to make the necessary changes in your life beginning today?

3. Have you completed you memory verse? *If not, do so today.*

4. Re-read the solution for worry in Philippians 4:6, 7. *Begin to apply it today.*

Honest Prayer (Communication) + Thanksgiving (Trust) = Peace that passes understanding

But He saith unto them, It is I; be not afraid. John 6:20

DAY 1—BEGIN IN PRAYER

1. Read John 6:22–40.

2. The discussion between Jesus and the crowd at Capernaum is quite similar to the conversation with the woman at the well. Read John 4:7–26, what do you notice about Jesus' example to us in meeting people right where they are and pointing out their spiritual need.

3. Look up the definition of the following words for a deeper understanding of their meaning.

   a. Seek (v. 26)

   b. Labor (v. 27)

   c. Perishes (v. 27)

   d. Will (v. 40)

4. Choose a verse to memorize this week and begin working on it now.

DAY 2—BEGIN IN PRAYER

1. Read John 6:22–40.

2. Re-read John 6:22–27.

3. The next morning those who had seen the miracles of Jesus, but had their eyes on the miracles instead of the miracle-worker, awoke to find Him missing and they set about to find Him. There is a correct motive and many incorrect motives for seeking Jesus early. What do we learn about the correct reason to seek Him?

a. 1Chronicles 28:9

b. Psalms 63:1–5

c. Proverbs 8:17

d. Matthew 6:33

4. The crowds sought Jesus because they had been given dinner. He knew what was in their hearts. Sometimes, as believers, we seek Jesus for the wrong reasons. What reminders do we get from the following Scriptures to help us check our motives?

a. Jeremiah 17:10

b. Jeremiah 23:23, 24

c. Hebrews 4:13

d. 1John 3:20

5. Jesus tells the crowd (and us) that we must not labor for meat that perishes but for that which endures unto everlasting life. How are we instructed to labor spiritually?

a. Isaiah 55:1–3

b. 1Corinthians 15:58

c. 2Timothy 4:5–7

d. Hebrews 12:1, 2

6. What specific lessons did you learn today? *(Truths to depend on; promises to believe; warnings to heed; examples to follow / not follow.)*

7. Write these lessons in the form of a question to yourself. *(What should I do? What should I not be doing? Do I truly believe these truths? Do I need to make any changes?)*

DAY 3—BEGIN IN PRAYER *(Don't forget Who the Teacher is!)*

1.   Read John 6:22–40.

2.   Re-read John 6:28–33.

3.   The crowd quickly misunderstood what Jesus was saying to them. Jesus spoke of spiritual *labor* and they wanted to know what *work* they could do to get to God. Our salvation is not a result of good living or right rules to follow, it comes only through faith in the One who was sent from Heaven. What truths and reminders do we find to keep us from falling into the trap of wanting to work our way to the Father?

     a. Romans 3:20

     b. Galatians 2:16

     c. Ephesians 2:8, 9

     d. Titus 3:4, 5

4.   Only one thing is required to be saved. Verse 29 is a concise description of salvation. We must believe on Him Who God hath sent. Use the following references to make this truth a reality deep in your heart.

     a. John 10:7–11

     b. Acts 4:10–12

c. Titus 2:13, 14

d. Hebrews 7:25

5. The Jewish crowd seeking "another sign" pointed to the provision of manna in the desert. Jesus used this to teach them of the true bread that not only "sustains" life, but gives eternal life and provides complete satisfaction. What promises are given to those who are His children?

a. John 10:10

b. 2Corinthians 9:8

c. Philippians 4:19

d. 1John 5:12, 13

6. What specific lessons did you learn today? *(Truths to depend on; promises to believe; warnings to heed; examples to follow / not follow.)*

7. Write these lessons in the form of a question to yourself. *(What should I do? What should I not be doing? Do I truly believe these truths? Do I need to make any changes?)*

DAY 4—BEGIN IN PRAYER

1. Read John 6:22–40. *(It really is important!)*

2. Re-read John 6:34–36.

3. The crowd with the spiritual blindness of their hearts totally missed the message of truth. Like the woman at the well who asked for living water, these replied *"give us this bread."* The Lord answered with the first of the *"I AM"* statements of the Gospel of John. "**I AM** *THE BREAD OF LIFE."* List the other six references.

    a. John 8:12

    b. John 10:7

    c. John 10:11

    d. John 11:25

    e. John 14:6

    f. John 15:1

4. A personal response is needed to this proclamation of the truth. A hungry person can sit at a table filled with food, turn up his nose, leave the table and still be as hungry as when he came. Being near the bread doesn't bring satisfaction. What do these Scriptures teach us about true satisfaction and contentment in Jesus Christ?

a. Psalms 17:15

b. Psalms 107:8, 9

c. Isaiah 58:11, 12

d. Matthew 5:6

5. Seeing is not necessarily believing. Read Luke 16:19–31 and record a few details that are given that confirm this truth.

6. What specific lessons did you learn today? *(Truths to depend on; promises to believe; warnings to heed; examples to follow / not follow.)*

7. Write these lessons in the form of a question to yourself. *(What should I do? What should I not be doing? Do I truly believe these truths? Do I need to make any changes?)*

DAY 5—BEGIN IN PRAYER

1. Read John 6:22–40.

2. Re-read John 6:37–40.

3. The opportunity for salvation is offered to all, *"and him who comes to Me I will in no wise cast out."* Record this truth given to us through the following verses.

   a. Deuteronomy 4:29

   b. Acts 2:21

   c. Romans 10:13

   d. 2Peter 3:9

4. When we come to the Lord in faith, trusting the work of Jesus for our salvation, we can be confident that it is by grace we are saved and by grace we are "kept." What strength and comfort can we receive from the following promises?

   a. Genesis 28:15

   b. 2Timothy 1:12

   c. 1Peter 1:3–5

d. Jude 24, 25

"The idea that a person once saved can be lost again is foreign to Scripture. *'All which He hath given Me I shall lose none'* Jesus said. Not just the victorious ones or the virtuous ones, but all! This concept brings peace to the heart and joy to the soul." *John Phillips — Exploring the Gospel of John*

5. Eternal life, the present possession of every believer, is a guarantee. We have this promise, it is the will of the Father, that everyone which sees the Son and believes on Him will have everlasting life and will be raised up on the last day. Look up the following references to learn more about the resurrection.

   a. John 11:25, 26

   b. 2Corinthians 4:14

   c. 1Thessalonians 4:16

6. What specific lessons did you learn today? *(Truths to depend on; promises to believe; warnings to heed; examples to follow / not follow.)*

7. Write these lessons in the form of a question to yourself. *(What should I do? What should I not be doing? Do I truly believe these truths? Do I need to make any changes?)*

DAY 6—BEGIN IN PRAYER

1. Read John 6:22–40.

2. What specific lessons has the Lord taught you this week? *Are you seeking Him for the correct reasons? What are you laboring for? Do you fall into the trap of thinking you can earn right standing with the Lord? What is it that satisfies you? Are you able to tell someone how to be saved? Do you worry about losing your salvation? Are you trusting Jesus to keep you to the end?*

3. Have you completed your memory verse for this week? *If not, finish it today.*

And Jesus said unto them, I am the bread of life: he that cometh to Me shall never hunger; and he that believeth on Me shall never thirst. John 6:35

DAY 1—BEGIN IN PRAYER

1. Read John 6:41–71.

2. The Jews murmured because they thought they knew who Jesus was. But, it was obvious that they didn't. What similarities do you see with those in this crowd and those who reject Jesus today?

3. In verse 63 we find the key to this teaching that Jesus had given to the Jews and His disciples. Read it again, write it out here and keep it in mind as you complete your study this week.

4. We find a progression that is the pattern for those who follow Jesus with the wrong motives in these verses. Find the descriptive word(s) that shows the rejection of the Lord in each of the following verses.

    a. Verse 41

    b. Verse 52

    c. Verse 66

5. Choose a verse to memorize this week. Begin working on it now.

DAY 2—BEGIN IN PRAYER

1. Read John 6:41–71.

2. Re-read John 6:41–47.

3   The Lord's statement, *"For I came down from heaven,"* disturbed the religious leaders, for they knew it was a claim of deity. Sometimes people admire Jesus in some way all the while refusing to submit to Him. The result is that they

begin to murmur. This is the same reaction we have when we don't believe or trust the Lord. Record who does it, why, and the results of this undesirable attitude.

a. Numbers 14:27–30

b. Psalm 106:24, 25

c. 1Corinthians 10:10

d. Jude 1:16

4. Verses 44 and 45 teach us that a person cannot come to Jesus if he hasn't been *drawn* by the Father, *taught* by the Father, *heard* from the Father and *learned* from the Father. It is the work of the Father drawing us to Jesus and revealing Him to us. Research this further by recording what you learn from the following verses.

a. Matthew 11:25–27

b. Matthew 16:17

c. Galatians 1:13–16

d. 1Corinthians 2:9–12

5.   As believers, we have the promise of the Lord that He will teach us and make known His ways unto us. What do we learn about the work of the Holy Spirit in our lives in teaching, leading and reminding us of the things we have learned?

a. Ezekiel 36:26, 27

b. John 14:26

c. John 16:13–15

d. 1Corinthians 2:12, 13

6.   What specific lessons did you learn today? *(Truths to depend on; promises to believe; warnings to heed; examples to follow / not follow.)*

7.   Write these lessons in the form of a question to yourself. *(What should I do? What should I not be doing? Do I truly believe these truths? Do I need to make any changes?)*

DAY 3—BEGIN IN PRAYER *(Remember Who teaches you.)*

1. Read John 6:41–71.

2. Re-read John 6:48–59.

3. Jesus again speaks of Himself as *"The Bread of Life."* He was proclaiming Himself to be the spiritual bread that came down from heaven that satisfies completely and gives eternal life. He was telling them that the bread which was to be given for the life of the world was His flesh. Without His death and resurrection we would be required to pay the price for our sin. What more can we learn about the penalty for sin and Jesus' death that paid the price?

    a. Romans 5:17, 18

    b. Romans 6:23

    c. 1 Corinthians 15:21, 22

    d. Revelation 5:9

4. *"To eat of this living bread,"* means *to accept Jesus Christ into our lives and become united with Him.* We become united with Christ in two ways: 1). by believing in His death and resurrection; and 2). by devoting ourselves each day to living as He requires, depending on His teaching for guidance, and trusting the Holy Spirit for power.

    Personal: According to this definition, are you united with Christ?

    What do we learn about how to know Jesus more intimately and how to be able to do the things He requires of us?

a. Psalm 19:7–10

b. John 14:23, 24

c. 1Peter 2:2

d. Philippians 2:13

5. Jesus points to His relationship with the Father as a model of the union He would share with us. As He depended on the Father for His life and lives because of the Father, so our we to have the same dependent relationship with Jesus. Record the truths you learn from the following verses.

a. John 15:4, 5

b. 2Corinthians 12:9, 10

c. Philippians 4:13

d. James 1:17

6. What specific lessons did you learn today? *(Truths to depend on; promises to believe; warnings to heed; examples to follow / not follow.)*

7. Write these lessons in the form of a question to yourself. *(What should I do? What should I not be doing? Do I truly believe these truths? Do I need to make any changes?)*

DAY 4—BEGIN IN PRAYER

1. Read John 6:41–71.

2. Re-read John 6:60–65.

3. The disciples were forced to examine their reasons for following Jesus and to test the depths of their commitment. John clearly tells us this problem of acceptance was among the disciples. Read the following parable and list the reasons that the seed of the Word of God doesn't bring forth fruit.

    a. Matthew 13:3–9

    b. Matthew 13:18–23

4. Jesus knew that the disciples were struggling, He asked, *"Does this offend you?"* or "cause you to stumble." The Greek word for *stumble (skandalizo)* is used often in the New Testament to speak of *falling away in unbelief.* Jesus was well aware that those who were not ready to believe in Him would stumble over Him or be offended by Him. What do the following references teach us about this stumbling block?

a. Mark 6:3–6

b. Romans 9:32, 33

c. 1Corinthians 1:23

d. 1Peter 2:7, 8

5. Jesus gives us the key to this dialogue, *"the words I speak to you they are spirit, and they are life. The flesh profits nothing."* The Word is spiritual and it is the Spirit that *quickens (brings life)*. When we seek to share the Lord and His Word with others we must remember the Word brings life and the Spirit draws men. Nothing we can do on our own will accomplish a spiritual work. Study these Scriptures to teach and remind you of this truth.

a. 2Corinthians 3:5, 6

b. Romans 10:17

c. Hebrews 4:12

d. 1Peter 1:23

6.   What specific lessons did you learn today? *(Truths to depend on; promises to believe; warnings to heed; examples to follow / not follow.)*

7.   Write these lessons in the form of a question to yourself. *(What should I do? What should I not be doing? Do I truly believe these truths? Do I need to make any changes?)*

DAY 5—BEGIN IN PRAYER

1.   Read John 6:41–71.

2.   Re-read John 6:66–71.

3.   Many chose to walk away. It is heart-breaking when one who appears to have known the Lord turns and walks away. The proof of true discipleship is endurance until the end. Record what you learn from these verses regarding the true disciple.

     a. Matthew 24:9–13

     b. Luke 8:15

     c. Hebrews 3:6

d. Revelation 2:10, 11

4. There is only **one way** to eternal life. Peter made an absolute statement, *"to Whom shall we go, Thou alone hast the words of eternal life."* Jesus is our life, He is our everything. If we are true disciples we will be positive there is nowhere else we would ever want to be. Do these Scriptures echo the cry of your heart?

     a. Psalm 16:11

     b. Psalm 17:15

     c. Psalm 42:1, 2

     d. Psalm 73:25, 26

5. Even in the midst of the disciples there was one who would betray the Lord. Jesus knew this from the beginning and yet He continued to love that one who followed for the wrong reasons and fooled everyone—but not Him. What warnings do we find regarding the wolves in the midst of the sheep?

     a. Matthew 7:15–17

     b. Colossians 2:8–10

c. 2Peter 3:17

d. Jude 1:4

6.   What specific lessons did you learn today? *(Truths to depend on; promises to believe; warnings to heed; examples to follow / not follow.)*

7.   Write these lessons in the form of a question to yourself. *(What should I do? What should I not be doing? Do I truly believe these truths? Do I need to make any changes?)*

DAY 6—BEGIN IN PRAYER *(Don't forget.)*

1.   Read John 6:41–71.

2.   What specific lessons has the Lord taught you this week? Jesus tested the faith of the disciples, how did you do? *Do you have a problem with murmuring when you don't understand or agree? Are you carefully listening to the guidance of the Holy Spirit? Is there a certain area that is not one with Christ? Anything choking out the seed of the Word? Do you ever long for "the old life" or are you convinced, with Peter, that there is no place else to go?*

3.   Have you completed your memory verse this week? *If not, do so today.*

*Thy Word have I hid in mine heart, that I might not sin against Thee.
Psalm 119:11*

*It is the spirit that quickeneth; the flesh profiteth nothing: the words
that I speak unto you, they are spirit, and they are life. John 6:63*

DAY 1 —BEGIN IN PRAYER

1. Read John 7:1–31.

2. From this chapter forward, John begins to show us the rejection and opposition to Jesus' ministry. By portraying Jesus' rejection, John gives us a realistic picture of the costs of being a true disciple. What has being a Christian *cost* you?

3. The events of this chapter take place during the Feast of the Tabernacles. What do you learn about this feast from the following Scriptures?

    a. Leviticus 23:34–44

    b. Deuteronomy 16:13–17

4. Choose a verse to memorize this week. Begin working on it now.

DAY 2—BEGIN IN PRAYER

1. Read John 7:1–31.

2. Re-read John 7:1–5.

3. There is a space of time between chapters 6 and 7 of approximately six months. Jesus had spent this time ministering in the Galilee area. He was well aware of the plot to kill Him (John 5) and it was not yet "His time" to die. This is the last time that Jesus spent in Galilee. He now begins His journey to the

cross. It was for this reason He had come, that we might have life. What clear picture do you get as you record the following Scriptures of Jesus' mission?

a. Isaiah 49:6, 7

b. Isaiah 53:1–12

c. Mark 8:31

d. Hebrews 12:2, 3

4. Notice that John refers to the feast as *"the Jews feast of the tabernacles,"* this was no longer the celebration of those who honored and loved God, but a religious ritual with no heart toward God. True discipleship, true honor and worship of God is measured by the obedience and joy in which service and worship are conducted. Obedience can be extremely expensive. What is the cost of true discipleship?

a. Matthew 16:24

b. Luke 14:26
(Note: Hate is a comparison word meaning that we are to first love the Lord above all else including mother, father, husband, and if ever there be a choice between the two, as disciples, we will chose the Lord.)

c. Luke 14:33

d. Luke 18:29, 30

5. Notice the word *"if"* in verse 4, Jesus' brothers tell Him, *"if"* you do these things you ought to go to Jerusalem and show thyself to the world. And John gives us the insight in verse 5, *"For neither did His brethren believe Him."* We often think that we can win others to Christ by our lifestyle and it is not necessary to speak to them. This should teach us that even the perfect life (Jesus') did not bring salvation. After Jesus' death and resurrection, we find Mary and His brethren in the upper room (Acts 1). It was His death and resurrection that convinced them of His deity. What method then should we use in sharing with those we know who are lost?

a. Acts 1:8

b. Romans 1:16

c. Hebrews 4:12

d. 1Thessalonians 1:5

6. What specific lessons did you learn today? *(Truths to depend on; promises to believe; warnings to heed; examples to follow / not follow.)*

7.   Write these lessons in the form of a question to yourself. *(What should I do? What should I not be doing? Do I truly believe these truths? Do I need to make any changes?)*

DAY 3—BEGIN IN PRAYER

1.   Read John 7:1–31.

2.   Re-read John 7:6–13.

3.   Jesus knew the spiritual climate in Jerusalem and He was working according to a divine timetable. He knew exactly when He was to go and He lived His life according to the plan set for Him. Jesus lived in moment to moment awareness of the will of the Father, in stark contrast to His brothers. As disciples, we, too, are to yield our lives to the Father's plan and listen for His still, small voice for direction moment by moment. What reminders do we find in these verses?

a. Psalm 25:8–10

b. Proverbs 3:5, 6

c. Isaiah 30:21

d. Isaiah 42:16

4.   The world does not hate those who are a part of themselves. It rejects those who do not belong to its system of rejection of God. The world rejected and

hated Jesus and therefore, it only follows that it will also reject those who follow Him. The Bible   many warnings and much comfort to those who find themselves outcast. What reminders do you find in these verses?

a. Matthew 5:10–12

b. John 15:18–20

c. John 17:14–16 (Jesus' prayer for us.)

d. 1John 3:1–13

5. After His brethren were well on their way Jesus went up to Jerusalem, but not openly. The discussion amongst the people was regarding who Jesus was. Was He a good man or a deceiver? The question is the same today, Who do you think Jesus is? He cannot be a *good man* without being God, because He filled the Bible with references of being equal with the Father. Some in the crowd believed that He was the Messiah but did not speak out for fear of the Jews. We cannot be secret disciples. We must follow all—or nothing! What clear direction do we find in the following references?

a. Proverbs 29:25

b. Matthew 10:32, 33

c. John 12:42, 43

d. 1John 4:14–16

6. What specific lessons did you learn today? *(Truths to depend on; promises to believe; warnings to heed; examples to follow / not follow.)*

7. Write these lessons in the form of a question to yourself. *(What should I do? What should I not be doing? Do I truly believe these truths? Do I need to make any changes?)*

DAY 4—BEGIN IN PRAYER

1. Read John 1:1–31.

2. Re-read John 1:14–24.

3. About midway through the feast, word spread that Jesus had come and was teaching boldly in the temple. Now the debate switched from His character to His doctrine. By the standards of the Pharisees, Jesus lacked credentials. He had not been to any schools, yet it was said that He taught with great authority. Jesus explained that His doctrine came directly from the Father. What do we learn from the following verses about the source of true wisdom?

    a. 2Chronicles 1:6–12

    b. Psalm 111:10

    c. 1Corinthians 2:6–13

    d. Colossians 2:2, 3

4.   John 7:17 literally reads, *"if any man is willing to do His* (God's) *will, he shall know."* How do we truly learn what God wants us to know? *By doing it.* God will reveal Himself to those who seek Him. This explains why these religious leaders could not see who Jesus was, they were not seeking Him. What does the Word promise to true seekers?

    a. 1Chronicles 28:9

    b. Psalm 145:18–20

    c. Isaiah 55:6, 7

    d. Matthew 7:7, 8

5.   This anger and hatred had begun more than a year earlier when Jesus healed the lame man on the Sabbath (John 5:16–18). The underlying cause of the Jewish hostility was that Jesus refused to bow to their rules and regulations concerning the Sabbath. They were willing to suspend the law of the Sabbath for the rite of circumcision, yet condemned Jesus for healing this man on the Sabbath. The question was a matter of righteous judgment. Study the following verses to find out more about righteous judgment.

a. Deuteronomy1:13–18

b. Proverbs 17:15

c. Proverbs 24:23

d. James 2:1–9

6. What specific lessons did you learn today? *(Truths to depend on, promises to believe, warnings to heed, examples to follow / not follow.)*

7. Write these lessons in the form of a question to yourself. *(What should I do? What should I not be doing? Do I truly believe these truths? Do I need to make any changes?)*

DAY 5—BEGIN IN PRAYER

1. Read John 7:1–31.

2. Re-read John 7:25–31.

3. There was some confusion in the crowds. They knew that the leaders sought

to kill Jesus yet there He was and no one arrested Him. The indecision of the authorities was not because of doubt, but a lack of opportunity. The last thing they wanted to do was incite a popular uprising. The question was, "where was the Messiah to come from?" They *felt* they knew who Jesus was and where He came from, but they didn't know His true Father so they *couldn't* know the Son. There is no room for neutrality when it comes to our relationship with the Lord. What truths do we learn about *total* commitment?

a. Luke 11:23

b. Revelation 3:15, 16

4. Jesus loudly cried, *"I am not come of Myself, and He that sent Me is true, Whom you know not. But I know Him: for I am from Him, and He hath sent Me."* Jesus was publicly declaring His Divine origin and the results infuriated the Jewish leaders to the point of action. This was the first attempt at arrest but His hour had not yet come. Record the future references for a better picture of the opposition Jesus faced.

a. John 8:59

b. John 10:31

c. John 10:39

d. John 11:57

5.　They could not arrest Jesus until it was God's perfect time and nothing or no one can prevent God's will from being accomplished. When we belong to God nothing comes into our lives that God does not allow. What reminders do we get from the following Scriptures?

　　a. Job 1:8–12

　　b. Psalm 34:7

　　c. Psalm 125:2

6.　What specific lessons did you learn today? *(Truths to depend on; promises to believe; warnings to heed; examples to follow / not follow.)*

7.　Write these lessons in the form of a question to yourself. *(What should I do? What should I not be doing? Do I truly believe these truths? Do I need to make any changes?)*

DAY 6—BEGIN IN PRAYER

1.   Read John 7:1–31. *(Don't cheat, it will become part of your life.)*

2.   What specific lessons has the Lord taught you this week?

Have you truly counted the cost? Are you willing to sacrifice all? What kind of witness have you been to your family? Is your time the Father's or your own?

Have you experienced any rejection because of following Jesus?

*Are you obediently following? Are you hot or cold—luke warm is **not good**?*

Do not leave any of these changes undone, allow the Lord to do His awesome, healing work today.

3.   Have you completed your memory verse this week? *If not, do so now.*

If any man will do His will, he shall know of the doctrine, whether it be of God, or whether I speak of Myself. John 7:17

DAY 1—BEGIN IN PRAYER

1. Read John 7:32–53.

2. The hostility has been steadily increasing against Jesus and His ministry. What two verses speak again of plans for arrest? What was the end result of these plans?

3. There were three types of listeners in this crowd that heard Jesus speak. Describe them in a few words.

    a. Verses 40–41a

    b. Verse 41b–42

    c. Verse 44

4. Choose a verse to memorize this week. Begin working on it now.

DAY 2—BEGIN IN PRAYER

1. Read John 7:32–53.

2. Re-read John 7: 32–36.

3. The debate among the people began to reach the ears of the Pharisees. The fact that many believed caused the Chief Priests to move, sending the temple officers to arrest Jesus. This is the first *official* attempt at arresting Him. Jesus spoke to them about the brevity of time in which they could come to Him. What more do we learn about the *"time of salvation"*?

a. Isaiah 49:8–10

b. 2Corinthians 6:2

c. Hebrew 3:7–14

4. To this mixed multitude of listeners Jesus says, *"you shall seek Me, and shall not find Me: and where I am, you cannot come."* What is different about the following passage when Jesus is speaking to His disciples?

    John 13:33–36.

5. What hope and encouragement do you receive from the following verses that describe our heavenly home and what difference do they make in how you live today?

    a. John 14:1–3

    b. John 17:24

    c. 1Thessalonians 4:16, 17

d. Revelation 3:21, 22

6. What specific lessons did you learn today? *(Truths to depend on; promises to believe; warnings to heed; examples to follow / not follow.)*

7. Write these lessons in the form of a question to yourself. *(What should I do? What should I not be doing? Do I truly believe these truths? Do I need to make any changes?)*

DAY 3—BEGIN IN PRAYER

1. Read John 7:32–53. *(This will help you to remember much better.)*

2. Re-read John 7:37–44.

3. The last day of the Feast was a special day, a holy solemn day, according to Leviticus 23:36 and Numbers 29:35. Along with instructions for keeping the Feast of Tabernacles given in the Old Testament, the Jews had added another *"tradition"* to the celebration. For seven days they circled the temple with a golden pitcher filled with water and poured it out on the steps of the temple. It was on this day Jesus stood and cried, saying, *"If any man thirst, let him come unto Me to drink."* What does God's Word reveal about the satisfaction of thirst?

    a. Psalm 36:7, 8

b. Matthew 5:6

c. John 4:14

d. Revelation 22:17

4. Jesus tells us that as believers we will have living water flowing from the innermost depths of our lives. John gives us the commentary, *"He spoke of the Spirit."* What do we learn about the living water of the Holy Spirit and its effect on our lives?

a. Joel 2:28, 29

b. Luke 11:13

c. Luke 24:49

d. Acts 1:8

5. Some believed, some argued, and some became very angry and hateful. When this division occurs as the result of preaching the Gospel, how are we to respond? Use the response of the following men as your example.

a. Peter and John — Acts 4:13–33

b. Stephen — Acts 7:51–60

c. Paul and Silas — Acts 16:20–25

6.   What specific lessons did you learn today? *(Truths to depend on; promises to believe; warnings to heed; examples to follow / not follow.)*

7.   Write these lessons in the form of a question to yourself. *(What should I do? What should I not be doing? Do I truly believe these truths? Do I need to make any changes?)*

DAY 4—BEGIN IN PRAYER

1.   Read John 7:32–53.

2.   Re-read John 7:45–49.

3.   The officers who were sent out to arrest Jesus returned empty handed. The reason, *"never man spoke like this Man."* They were amazed at the authority. It was evident that the words He spoke were God's. The power of God's Words that these men witnessed is the very same today. What do we learn about the power of God's Word and how do these verses help when we are tempted to look for answers elsewhere?

a. Isaiah 55:11

b. Jeremiah 23:29

c. 2Corinthians 10:4, 5

d. Hebrews 4:12, 13

4.   The Pharisees responded with pride and arrogance because they *thought* they were much better than the common people. The Bible gives us very clear teachings about this attitude and we need to be aware because it can sometimes creep into the church. What do we learn about pride and the ugliness it brings with it?

a. Proverbs 11:2

b. Proverbs 16:18

c. Obadiah 1:3, 4

d. James 4:6

5. We need to beware of the attitude of the world that would have us to believe that wisdom comes from learning, education and training within the world system. The Bible teaches us that wisdom comes from the Lord. What do these Scriptures tell us about worldly wisdom and those who practice it?

a. Isaiah 44:24, 25

b. Romans 1:21, 22

c. 1Corinthians 1:19–21

d. 1Corinthians 3:18, 19

6. What specific lessons did you learn today? *(Truths to depend on; promises to believe; warnings to heed; examples to follow / not follow.)*

7. Write these lessons in the form of a question to yourself. *(What should I do? What should I not be doing? Do I truly believe these truths? Do I need to make any changes?)*

DAY 5—BEGIN IN PRAYER

1. Read John 7:32–53.

2. Re-read John 7:50–53.

3. The Pharisees had just received the testimony of some unwanted witnesses, the soldiers, and now speaks the one who had come to Jesus by night. Review John 3:1–21 and record a few details of the meeting between Nicodemus and Jesus.

   What do you think it cost Nicodemus, *who was one of them,* to speak out on behalf of Jesus?

4. The Pharisees were judging Jesus before they knew the facts. They did not know Jesus or where He was born, yet they had passed judgment and would not hear anything more about Him. We need to be careful not to fall into judgment of others on hearsay or half truths. What reminders do we find in the following references about judging one another?

   a. Proverbs 18:13

   b. Luke 6:37

   c. Romans 14:10–13

   d. James 4:11, 12

5. In the face of the opposition that these who believed faced, could you prove why you believe that Jesus is the Son of God? The Bereans searched the Scriptures to find out if what they were being taught was true (Acts 17:11). *If you cannot answer "yes," it is time to become like the Bereans. You may want to purchase and study a book such as "Know Why You Believe" by Paul Little.*

    Challenge: Try finding three verses that you would share to prove that Jesus is the Messiah.

    a.

    b.

    c.

6. What specific lessons did you learn today? *(Truths to depend on; promises to believe; warnings to heed; examples to follow / not follow.)*

7. Write these lessons in the form of a question to yourself. *(What should I do? What should I not be doing? Do I truly believe these truths? Do I need to make any changes?)*

DAY 6 —BEGIN IN PRAYER

1.   Read John 7:32–53.

2.   What specific lessons has the Lord taught you this week? What areas in your life has He shown you need to let Him make changes? *Does your heart long for your heavenly home? Are you truly satisfied? Do you see the power of the Holy Spirit in your life? How do you respond to hostility to the Gospel? Are you ever tempted to be filled with pride? Do you look to the "wisdom of the world" for answers to your problems? Are you quick to judge? Could you tell someone "why" you believe?*

Seek the Lord in prayer and allow Him to make the changes necessary in your life. Use your concordance to look up more Scriptures in any area that the Lord has spoken to you about this week.

3.   Have you completed you memory verse this week? *If not, do so today.*

The officers answered, Never man spake like this Man. John 7:46

DAY 1—BEGIN IN PRAYER

1. Read John 8:1–30.

2. Re-read John 8:1–30 and record the references Jesus makes of Himself as the *"I AM."*

3. Look up the definitions of the following words to help you get a better understanding of these teachings.

    a. Verse 7 - Without sin

    b. Verse 11 - Condemn

    c. Verse 12 - Light

    d. Verse 24 - Die

4. Choose a verse to memorize this week. Begin working on it now.

DAY 2—BEGIN IN PRAYER

1. Read John 8:1–30.

2. Re-read John 8:1–11.

3.   Jesus had left the night before to go to the Mt. of Olives, but here we find Him early in the morning teaching in the temple. His listeners desired to hear the truth, but Jesus' enemies sought to catch Him in a trap. What do we learn from the following verses about the plans and snares of the enemy?

a. Luke 12:45, 46

b. 1 Peter 5:8, 9

c. 1 Timothy 6:9, 10

d. 2 Timothy 2:25, 26

4.   These accusers were not interested in justice or the law, only the public discrediting of Jesus. However, Jesus used the plan of His enemies to teach a very important lesson—that all have sinned and God's judgment is surrounded in mercy. What do we learn about the mercy of God from the following Scriptures?

a. Psalm 103:17

b. Lamentations 3:22, 23

c. Micah 7:18

d. Titus 3:5

5. When all of this woman's accusers left, *"convicted by their own conscience,"* this woman was left alone with the Lord. The crowd was gone, but condemnation was not gone. The only one who could cast the stone was Jesus; He didn't. He offered her forgiveness. Notice that forgiveness is not without responsibility. Repentance (180° change of direction) and obedience are true marks of the one who receives God's forgiveness. What direction do we find about how our lives must be lived because we have been forgiven?

a. Isaiah 55:7

b. John 5:14

c. Romans 6:12, 13

d. Ephesians 4:22–24

6. What specific lessons did you learn today? *(Truths to depend on; promises to believe; warnings to heed; examples to follow / not follow.)*

7.　Write these lessons in the form of a question to yourself. *(What should I do? What should I not be doing? Do I truly believe these truths? Do I need to make any changes?)*

DAY 3—BEGIN IN PRAYER

1.　Read John 8:1–30.

2.　Re-read John 8:12–18.

3.　As Jesus spoke, He was near the temple treasury (v. 20) which was included in the court of the women. There is a huge candelabra located in this area used during the feast of Tabernacles to represent and remind the worshippers of God's leading in the wilderness in the pillar of fire. Jesus declares: *"I AM the light of the world."* This is the second of Jesus' *"I AM"* statements recorded in the Gospel of John. What more can we learn about the Light of the World?

　　a. Isaiah 9:2

　　b. John 1:1–4

　　c. John 12:35, 36

　　d. 2Corinthians 4:6

4.   What responsibilities do we have as believers who are walking in the light?

a. Matthew 5:14–16

b. Romans 13:12–14

c. Ephesians 5:8–10

d. Philippians 2:14–16

5.   The Pharisees couldn't kill Jesus nor could they trap Him, so they tried to use the law to discredit Him. By Jewish law, two witnesses were required as proof of any truth. The Pharisees declared that Jesus' statement of Himself was not true because He had no other witnesses. They judged by what they *could not* know (because they walked in darkness). What do we learn about judging and judgment and how should this effect our relationships with one another?

a. Matthew 7:1

b. Romans 14:13

c. 2Timothy 4:8

d. Hebrews 12:23

6. What specific lessons did you learn today? *(Truths to depend on; promises to believe; warnings to heed; examples to follow / not follow.)*

7. Write these lessons in the form of a question to yourself. *(What should I do? What should I not be doing? Do I truly believe these truths? Do I need to make any changes?)*

DAY 4 - BEGIN IN PRAYER *(Don't forget Who your Teacher is.)*

1. Read John 8:1–30.

2. Re-read John 8:19–24.

3. In these verses we find the ultimate contrast between light and darkness. Record the stark differences found in the following verses.

    a. **Verse 19**
    Light:

    Darkness:

    b. **Verse 21**
    Light:

    Darkness:

    c. **Verse 23**
    Light:

    Darkness:

4.   The Pharisees resorted to name calling, "Where is your father?"(See verse 41.) Jesus' response, *"ye neither know Me, nor My Father: if you had known Me, ye should have known My Father also."* Those who are His know Him, those who refuse cannot hear His voice. What insight do we get about the Shepherd and His sheep?

     a. Psalm 23:1

     b. Isaiah 40:11

     c. John 10:2–5

     d. John 10:14–16

5.   Instead of hearing, they began to argue amongst themselves. Jesus declares His deity. He is from above and without faith in Him they would die in their sins. The wages of sin is death. *"For if you believe not that I AM,"* the results of that unbelief are eternal. There is only one way to escape. What do we learn about the way to heaven? How can memorizing these verses help you when you daily meet those who are dying in their sins?

     a. John 3:16

     b. Acts 4:12

     c. Romans 10:9, 10; 13

d. Revelation 22:17

6. What specific lessons did you learn today? *(Truths to depend on; promises to believe; warnings to heed; examples to follow / not follow.)*

7. Write these lessons in the form of a question to yourself. *(What should I do? What should I not be doing? Do I truly believe these truths? Do I need to make any changes?)*

DAY 5—BEGIN IN PRAYER

1. Read John 8:1–30. *(It's important!)*

2. Re-read John 8:25–30.

3. The argument continues with the Pharisees asking, *"Who art Thou?"* They didn't really want to know. Just as with these, there are many today who will not hear. Record the description of their blinded, hardened hearts.

    a. Isaiah 59:8

    b. Jeremiah 5:4

    c. Romans 10:3

d. Ephesians 4:18

4.   Knowing the difference between the way we, as believers, view the world and the way those who are part of the world see things, what direction do we get in order to make a difference in the darkness?

a. 2Corinthians 10:3–5

b. Galatians 6:10–18

c. 1John 5:4

5.   Jesus declares that His Father had not left Him alone; for He does always those things which please the Father. We need to use our Lord's example as a daily reminder that we are never alone and filter every thought and action through this question, *"Does this please the Father?"* What further encouragement do we get from the following Scriptures to please Him?

a. Proverbs 16:7

b. Micah 6:8

c. 1Thessalonians 2:4

d. 1 Thessalonians 4:1

6. What specific lessons did you learn today? *(Truths to depend on; promises to believe; warnings to heed; examples to follow / not follow.)*

7. Write these lessons in the form of a question to yourself. *(What should I do? What should I not be doing? Do I truly believe these truths? Do I need to make any changes?)*

DAY 6—BEGIN IN PRAYER

1. Read John 8:1–30.

2. What specific lessons have you learned this week? Review Question #7 of days 2–5. *How are you doing?*

    Spend some time in prayer *right now* asking the Lord to make these changes and surrendering your will to Him that He will be able to transform your life.

3. Have you completed your memory verse for this week? *If not, finish it today.*

    Then spake Jesus again unto them, saying, I am the light of the world: He that followeth Me shall not walk in darkness, but shall have the light of life. John 8:12

DAY 1—BEGIN IN PRAYER

1. Read John 8:31–59.

2. Re-read John 8:31–59 and record what Jesus says **about Himself** and **His Words**. Be sure to give the references for your answers.

3. Look up the definition of the following words to learn more about their meaning.

    a. Continue (v. 31)

    b. Free (v. 32)

    c. Servant (v. 34)

    d. Verily (v. 51)

    e. Keep (v. 51)

4. Choose a verse to memorize this week. Begin working on it now.

Jesus
CHRIST
son of GOD

DAY 2—BEGIN IN PRAYER

1. Read John 8:31–59.

2. Re-read John 8:31–37.

3. There were some in this crowd that at least began to believe that it was possible that the statements Jesus made were true. The Lord gives them this measuring stick to judge their faith. True disciples are obedient and they remain faithful to the very end. What more do we learn about the true follower of Christ?

    a. Matthew 24:13

    b. Hebrews 3:14

    c. Hebrews 10:35–39

    d. James 1:25

4. Jesus declares to the world the source of absolute freedom. Freedom from sin, from death, from the bondage of the enemy and the world. When Jesus spoke of knowing the truth, He was speaking of knowing God's revelation to man. This revelation is embodied in Jesus Himself, therefore, to know Jesus is to know the truth. Absolute truth is found in God's Word. Record what lessons you find in the following Scriptures?

    a. Psalm 25:5–10

b. Psalm 119:9–11

c. John 17:17

d. Colossians 2:8–10

5.   Jesus uses the illustration of slavery to make this truth clear. A slave has no rights, power, privilege or inheritance in the master's home. However, the Son has all of these and the certainty that he will always be a part of the home. So it is with the one who is in bondage to sin, he is exactly like that slave, he is a servant to sin. Only through faith in the Son can we be made free from sin and death. What do we learn about this true freedom in Christ?

a. Romans 6:12–14

b. Romans 6:16–18

c. Galatians 5:1

d. Philippians 2:13

6.   What specific lessons did you learn today? *(Truths to depend on; promises to believe; warnings to heed; examples to follow / not follow.)*

7.   Write these lessons in the form of a question to yourself. *(What should I do? What should I not be doing? Do I truly believe these truths? Do I need to make any changes?)*

DAY 3—BEGIN IN PRAYER
(Don't forget this is the most important thing you can do!)

1.   Read John 8:31–59.

2.   Re-read John 8:38–44.

3.   These listening Jews took great exception to Jesus' comments and began to argue. Jesus made it clear to them that there was a great difference between Abraham's *seed* and Abraham's *spiritual children*. They claimed to be children of Abraham yet they sought to kill Jesus. They had a different *spiritual father*. What do we learn about Abraham's true children?

a. Genesis 18:18, 19

b. Acts 3:24–26

c. Romans 4:11–13

d. Galatians 3:7–9

4. These who claimed to be Abraham's children lived lives that did not back up their profession. As believers, we are not to behave as these who said one thing and did the opposite. What does the Bible say about the honesty and integrity of our witness?

a. Philippians 1:9–11

b. Philippians 1:27

c. Titus 2:7, 8

d. 1 Peter 2:12–15

5. There are two *families* described in these verses: one whose Father is God; the other whose father is the devil. Jesus came right out and told them this truth. They did not understand His speech because they *would not* hear. God's Word is revealed through the Spirit to those who truly seek Him. Those who refuse to come act according to the nature of their father. Record the character description of those who will not follow God.

a. Romans 1:21–32

b. 2 Timothy 3:1–5

c. 2Timothy 4:3

Are you surprised by the Nightly News? Pray for greater boldness to share the way to have true freedom from this life of bondage to sin!

6. What specific lessons did you learn today? *(Truths to depend on; promises to believe; warnings to heed; examples to follow / not follow.)*

7. Write these lessons in the form of a question to yourself. *(What should I do? What should I not be doing? Do I truly believe these truths? Do I need to make any changes?)*

DAY 4—BEGIN IN PRAYER

1. Read John 8:31–59.

2. Re-read John 8:45–50.

3. In contrast to the devil, who always lies, Jesus speaks only the truth. We can trust all that He says and we need not fear that He will fail us, because He always speaks the truth. Apply these following truths to the doubts in your life.

a. Deuteronomy 32:4

b. Psalm 146:6

c. Romans 3:4

d. Hebrews 6:18

4. In verse 47, Jesus tells us that he that is of God hears God's words. These could not hear because they were deaf as a result of being dead in their sins. There is more to hearing than simply allowing the words to bounce off an ear-drum. True spiritual hearing implies that the truths become a vital part of your life and the force that leads every thought and decision. *Are you truly hearing His Words?* Test your hearing with these Scriptures.

a. Matthew 7:16–20

b. Matthew 13:23

c. Acts 17:11

d. James 2:17–20

5. The crowd becomes even more hostile to Jesus and begins calling Him more names. Name calling usually indicates that a person has run out of intelligent comments. Notice that Jesus ignores the Samaritan comment and denies the truth of being demon possessed by referring them to His Father who will

find them and judge them for their unbelief. What lessons can we learn and appropriate in similar circumstances?

a. Mark 14:60, 61

b. Hebrews 12:2, 3

c. 1 Peter 2:21–24

d. 1 Peter 4:19

6.   What specific lessons did you learn today? *(Truths to depend on, promises to believe, warnings to heed, examples to follow / not follow.)*

7.   Write these lessons in the form of a question to yourself. *(What should I do? What should I not be doing? Do I truly believe these truths? Do I need to make any changes?)*

DAY 5—BEGIN IN PRAYER

1.   Read John 8:31–59. *(It is very important!)*

2.   Re-read John 8:51–59.

3. When the words *"Verily, verily"* precede a statement we need to know that this is a God-spoken, unshakable truth. *"If a man keeps My saying, he shall never see death."* This death spoken of by Jesus is spiritual death. What more can we learn from the teachings of the Bible regarding this truth?

    a. John 3:15, 16

    b. John 5:24

    c. John 11:25, 26

    d. 1John 5:11, 12

4. Those who continued to argue could not see the truth because they refused to hear. Jesus is not speaking of physical death. They again try to use Abraham and the prophets to argue against Jesus' claims but He tells them, at the expense of His life, He came to honor the Father. Jesus came and willingly laid down His life so that we could have life. His purpose was to honor the Father. As believers, we have the very same purpose. What specific direction do we get from the following references?

    a. Psalm 86:11–13

    b. Romans 15:5, 6

    c. Colossians 1:9–11

d. 1 Thessalonians 4:1–4

5. Take notice of the reaction of those who heard Jesus declare, *"Before Abraham was, I AM."* They took up stones to kill Him. They understood exactly what He was telling them. He was declaring that He was God. There are many today who say that Jesus was a *good man* yet that description denies His very description of Himself. He is either God or He was lying. How could you use these verses to speak to one who calls Jesus a *good man?*

What more can we learn about the eternal existence of Jesus?

a. John 1:1–4

b. Colossians 1:16, 17

c. Hebrews 1:10–12

6. What specific lessons did you learn today? *(Truths to depend on; promises to believe; warnings to heed; examples to follow / not follow.)*

7. Write these lessons in the form of a question to yourself. *(What should I do? What should I not be doing? Do I truly believe these truths? Do I need to make any changes?)*

DAY 6—BEGIN IN PRAYER

1. Read John 8:31–59.

2. What specific lessons has the Lord taught you this week? Are you willing to allow Him to make the changes that are necessary in your life and heart? *Is your life an example of a true follower of Christ? Are you totally convinced that absolute truth comes from God's Word alone? Are you experiencing true freedom? Does obedience or disobedience characterize your life?* Allow the Lord to make His desired changes in your life today.

Verily, verily, I say unto you, If a man keep My saying, he shall never see death. John 8:51

DAY 1—BEGIN IN PRAYER

1. Read John 9:1–41.

2. In John chapter 9, we begin a record of some of the fruit that resulted from Jesus' ministry. Even though the leaders continued in their darkness, many came to Jesus and were brought spiritually *"into the light."* Re-read John 9:1–41 and record the comments and reactions of each of these people to the miracle that Jesus performed. Be sure to give verse references for each of your answers.

    a. The Pharisees

    b. The Parents

    c. The Man Who Was Healed

3. How does this miracle illustrate that Jesus is *"the Light of the World"*?

4. Choose a verse to memorize this week. Begin working on it today.

DAY 2—BEGIN IN PRAYER

1. Read John 9:1–41.

2. Re-read John 9:1–7.

3. Jesus passed by and saw this man who was born blind. The disciples asked a universal question, "Why?" Jesus replied, it had a purpose. There are no pat

answers regarding suffering and tragedy that happens in our lives. There is one thing that we can be sure of, nothing can happen to us that is not allowed by our Heavenly Father. What comfort and encouragement can we draw from the following Scriptures?

a. Job 1:7–12

b. Psalm 34:6–8

c. Psalm 125:2

d. 1Corinthians 10:13

4. Jesus turned the disciples attention away from the cause to the purpose. This happened that the work of God might be displayed through this man's life. As Christians the very purpose of our lives is that God would be honored and glorified. Trials and suffering have a purpose of drawing us closer to, and making us be more dependent on, the Lord. What more can we learn about the correct perspective on suffering?

a. 2Corinthians 12:7–10

b. 1Peter 1:6, 7

c. 1Peter 4:12–14

d. James 1:2–4

5. Jesus finds this man and chose him to be healed (spiritually and physically). In the same manner, He found us when we were lost in our sin and healed us from spiritual death. We get an awesome picture of the Sovereignty of God from this account of the healing of the blind man. God is the One Who heals and He does so in His timing and according to His perfect plan. Record what you learn from the following references about healing.

a. Exodus 15:26

b. Job 5:17–22

c. Psalm 103:2–5

d. Psalm 147:2–5

6. What specific lessons did you learn today? *(Truths to depend on; promises to believe; warnings to heed; examples to follow / not follow.)*

7.   Write these lessons in the form of a question to yourself. *(What should I do? What should I not be doing? Do I truly believe these truths? Do I need to make any changes?)*

DAY 3—BEGIN IN PRAYER

1.   Read John 9:1–41.

2.   Re-read John 9:8–17.

3.   This miracle that had taken place in this man's life was hard for those who knew him to believe. Their response varied, maybe this was him or maybe not. Maybe he had not been born totally blind. However, it was very obvious to all who saw him that something miraculous had happened. So it is with one who accepts Jesus Christ as their Savior, the change in their lifestyle and outlook are transformed. What does God's Word tell us about this transformation?

a. Romans 8:29

b. 2Corinthians 3:18

c. 2Corinthians 5:17

d. Colossians 3:10

4. Those who questioned this formerly blind man kept asking *"how"* did this happen. It is not uncommon for mankind to seek a formula or a method instead of looking for a relationship with the One Who heals and restores. Christianity is not a religion (man trying to get to God), it is a relationship in which God came to us. It is this eternal truth Jesus is sharing with this man and any who will hear. What open invitation do we find regarding our intimate fellowship with the Lord?

   a. Isaiah 45:21, 22

   b. Matthew 11:28–30

   c. John 6:37

   d. Revelation 22:17

5. The Jewish Sabbath, Saturday, was the weekly holy day of rest. God had intended this day to be a day of rest and a day in which to honor and worship the Lord. The Pharisees had made a long list of specific do's and don'ts regarding the Sabbath that caused it to be almost impossible to keep. Jesus had healed this man on the Sabbath (not the first time—remember John 5:1–10) to teach that it is right to care for others' needs even on the Sabbath. Review the following verses regarding the Sabbath, *have you truly entered into the rest that Jesus provides, everyday?*

   a. Exodus 20:8–11

   b. Isaiah 58:13, 14

c. Mark 2:27, 28

d. Hebrews 4:1–10 *(Jesus is our "Sabbath" rest.)*

6. What specific lessons did you learn today? *(Truths to depend on; promises to believe; warnings to heed; examples to follow / not follow.)*

7. Write these lessons in the form of a question to yourself. *(What should I do? What should I not be doing? Do I truly believe these truths? Do I need to make any changes?)*

DAY 4—BEGIN IN PRAYER

1. Read John 9:1–41.

2. Re-read John 9:18–29.

3. Not surprisingly, the Pharisees didn't believe the testimony of this man. They called the man's parents in hopes that they would refute their own son's testimony. But because of the threats of the Pharisees toward anyone who confessed to believe in Jesus, they said he is our son, he was born blind and that's all we know. They feared what man could do to them and that same fear often keeps us from proclaiming Jesus as Savior and Lord. What encouragement do we find in these verses to stand boldly?

a. Psalm 118:8

b. Proverbs 29:25

c. Matthew 10:28–33

4.   To be put out of the synagogue meant not only religious isolation, it affected every part of the persons life—social, economical, and security. When we are called to follow Jesus, we are to count the cost and sometimes the cost is tremendous. Count the cost according to these following Scriptures.

a. Matthew 10:34–37

b. Matthew 16:24–26

c. Luke 9:57–62

d. Luke 14:26–28

5.   Again they called this man back to testify and He becomes a bolder witness with every question. He simply told them what he knew. He proclaims, *"I have told you already, and you did not hear: wherefore, would you hear it again? Will you also be His disciples?"* We are called to be witness in word and in deed. Find out where this boldness and power comes from in our lives.

a. Zechariah 4:6

b. Acts 1:8

c. 1Corinthians 2:4, 5

d. 1Thessalonians 1:5

6. What specific lessons did you learn today? *(Truths to depend on; promises to believe; warnings to heed; examples to follow / not follow.)*

7. Write these lessons in the form of a question to yourself. *(What should I do? What should I not be doing? Do I truly believe these truths? Do I need to make any changes?)*

DAY 5—BEGIN IN PRAYER

1. Read John 9:1–41.

2. Re-read John 9:30–41.

3. The Pharisees had decided not to believe and therefore had to make many irrational conclusions. They began with He must not be of God because He healed on the Sabbath and now, Who is He, we don't even know Him. Remember earlier they said, *"He can't be the Messiah, everyone knows where He comes from."* This *former blind man* begins to teach the *spiritually blind.*

He tells them we know that God does not hear sinners. There are many Scriptures that support this man's statement. Record what you learn from the following verses.

a. Job 27:8, 9

b. Psalms 66:18

c. Proverbs 15:29

d. Isaiah 59:2

4.   On the other hand, the eyes and the ears of the Lord are always open to those who love Him and are called by His name. What encouragement do you find in the following references?

a. 2Chronicles 7:14

b. Luke 18:1

c. 1Peter 3:12

d. James 5:16

5.   The man tells the Pharisees something that they should have known. The Scriptures clearly speak of the Messiah as the One Who would open the eyes of the blind. Record these prophecies and then you can understand why they cast him out of the synagogue.

a. Isaiah 29:18, 19

b. Isaiah 35:4–7

c. Isaiah 42:6–8

d. Psalm 146:8–10

Notice: Jesus found this man and totally revealed Himself to him. He believed and fell down and worshiped Him. Jesus readily accepted his worship. He had gone from physically and spiritually blind to spiritually and physically whole.

6.   What specific lessons did you learn today? *(Truths to depend on, promises to believe, warnings to heed, examples to follow / not follow.)*

7.   Write these lessons in the form of a question to yourself. *(What should I do? What should I not be doing? Do I truly believe these truths? Do I need to make any changes?)*

DAY 6—BEGIN IN PRAYER

1.   Read John 9:1–41.

2.   What specific lessons has the Lord taught you this week? Where do you find yourself in this account? Spend some time in prayer asking the Lord to teach you these lessons and make them a part of your everyday life.

3.   Have you completed your memory verse this week? *If not, do so today.*

I must work the works of Him that sent Me, while it is day: the night cometh, when no man can work. John 9:4

DAY 1—BEGIN IN PRAYER

1. Read John 10:1–21.

2. Re-read John 10:1-21 and record the characteristics of the Good Shepherd from the following references and explain what each one tells us about Jesus.

    a. John 10:2; 7

    b. John 10:4; 14

    c. John 10:10

    d. John 10:11

3. Paralleling leaders with shepherds and their people with sheep is a common analogy in the Bible and God is often called a shepherd of His people, the sheep. Record what you learn from the following references for a solid background to understand this parable and its application to us.

    a. Psalm 23:1

    b. Isaiah 40:10, 11

    c. Jeremiah 31:10

Jesus
CHRIST
son of GOD

d. 1 Peter 2:25

4.   Choose a verse to memorize this week. Begin working on it today. *(Remember, the Lord cannot bring to your memory what you have not memorized.)*

DAY 2—BEGIN IN PRAYER

1.   Read John 10:1–21.

2.   Re-read John 10:1–5.

3.   John chapter 10 focuses on the image of sheep, sheepfolds and shepherds. He begins by contrasting the good shepherd with the false shepherd. The sheepfold was the place that the sheep were kept at night for protection. It was built of stones or branches and had only one entrance at which the shepherd slept to protect the sheep. Speaking of the false teachers and leaders, those who didn't truly care for the sheep, Jesus characterizes them as thieves and robbers. What warnings do we find about the thief and robber who would seek to harm the sheep?

a. Matthew 7:15–20

b. Matthew 24:4, 5

c. Colossians 2:8

4.   The True Shepherd called His sheep out of the sheepfold (Judaism). They heard the voice of the Messiah and followed Him. This is exactly what happened to this blind man who had been healed, he heard, he followed, and he found life. What does God's Word say about those who truly belong to the Lord?

a. Proverbs 8:34, 35

b. John 6:37

c. 2Timothy 2:19

d. James 1:12

5.   The sheep of the Good Shepherd know His voice and they follow only Him. What does Psalm 23 teach us about the state of the sheep in the flock of the Good Shepherd?

6.   What specific lessons did you learn today? *(Truths to depend on; promises to believe; warnings to heed; examples to follow / not follow.)*

7.　Write these lessons in the form of a question to yourself. *(What should I do? What should I not be doing? Do I truly believe these truths? Do I need to make any changes?)*

DAY 3—BEGIN IN PRAYER

1.　Read John 10:1–21.

2.　Re-read John 10:6–10.

3.　As is so often seen, those who were listening did not understand this illustration that Jesus was teaching. He continues to give a more detailed account, but now He focuses our attention on those who have followed Him. He declares, *"I AM the door of the sheep,"* the only way in which man can enter into the flock of God and find eternal life. There is only one way for man to escape the trap of sin, that is by entering through the door unto salvation and eternal life. What do we learn about this *only door?*

a. John 14:6

b. Acts 4:12

c. Ephesians 2:14–19

d. 1 John 5:11–13

4. Notice the change of language in verse 9, *"I am the door; by Me if any man enter in, he shall be saved."* This is an even broader invitation than in verse 7, when He was speaking of the lost sheep of the house of Israel. The call goes out to *"whosoever will come."* And when they do, they experience the freedom and satisfaction that only Christ can offer. What do we learn and *how are you experiencing this freedom and satisfaction?*

    a. Psalm 65:4

    b. Proverbs 19:23

    c. John 8:36

    d. Galatians 5:1

5. Jesus declares that all who came before Him, but refused to acknowledge their need for a Savior, had no authority to claim that they could show man the way to enter into Heaven. Certainly He was including those Scribes and Pharisees who had banished this blind man because of his faith in Jesus. Their objective was *"to kill, steal and destroy."* Jesus offers abundant life to those who hear His voice and follow Him. What specifics can we learn about this abundant life that is ours in Christ?

    a. Psalm 36:7, 8

    b. 2Corinthians 9:8

c. Ephesians 3:20

d. Philippians 4:19

6.   What specific lessons did you learn today? *(Truths to depend on; promises to believe; warnings to heed; examples to follow / not follow.)*

7.   Write these lessons in the form of a question to yourself. *(What should I do? What should I not be doing? Do I truly believe these truths? Do I need to make any changes?)*

DAY 4—BEGIN IN PRAYER

1.   Read John 10:1–21.

2.   Re-read John 10:11–15.

3.   What do we find to be the most significant characteristic of the Good Shepherd?

a. Verse 11

b. Verse 15

c. Verse 17

d. Verse 18

4. The Good Shepherd *"gives His life for the sheep."* The word for *gives* is usually translated *"lays down"* and *"for the sheep"* signifies, on their behalf. Therefore, the Good Shepherd gave His life freely and voluntarily in the place of His people, as a ransom for them, that they might be delivered from death and receive eternal life. What do these Scriptures add to remind us of this awesome truth?

a. Isaiah 53:4–6

b. Ephesians 5:2

c. Titus 2:13, 14

d. 1Peter 2:21–25

5. List the description of a hireling according to verses 12 and 13. How does this description sadly compare to some who call themselves shepherds (pastors) today? What warnings do we find to those pastors, to those who would minister to others, and to every sheep?

a. Ezekiel 34:2–6

b. Zechariah 11:17

c. Acts 20:29–31

d. 2Peter 2:1–3

6. What specific lessons did you learn today? *(Truths to depend on; promises to believe; warnings to heed; examples to follow / not follow.)*

7. Write these lessons in the form of a question to yourself. *(What should I do? What should I not be doing? Do I truly believe these truths? Do I need to make any changes?)*

DAY 5—BEGIN IN PRAYER

1. Read John 10:1–21.

2. Re-read John 10:16–21.

3. These other sheep that Jesus is speaking of were those who were outside of Judaism. They were the Gentiles to which the Gospel would be taken. The Good News of salvation was to go into all the world. Jesus says, *"them also I must bring."* We gain insight into the process of coming to the Lord from this statement. It is the Holy Spirit that draws the hearts of men to the Lord. Record the details you gather from the following references.

a. Jeremiah 31:3

b. John 6:44

c. John 6:65

d. John 12:32, 33

4. These sheep from the fold of Judaism and the Gentile believers were to be one flock. This was a concept that was foreign to the Jews because of their very deep seated religious pride. (Remember Peter in Acts 10? If not, review this account.) Jesus lays down a truth that we need to live by and yet it is challenged daily by our flesh and the enemy. What do we learn from the following Scriptures about unity in the Body of Christ and our responsibility to maintain it?

a. Romans 12:5

b. 1 Corinthians 1:10

c. Galatians 3:28

d. 1 Peter 3:8, 9

5. No man took Jesus' life from Him, He willingly laid it down and Jesus declared that He had power to raise Himself from the dead. This statement astounded those who were listening and a division resulted *again.* He declared that He was God and proof of that truth is that He had power over life and death. Jesus rose from the dead so that death would be conquered and that we could have entrance into heaven. What does the Bible teach us about death and the believer?

    a. Psalm 116:15

    b. 1 Corinthians 15:51–57

    c. 1 Thessalonians 4:14–17

    d. 1 Thessalonians 5:9–11

6. What specific lessons did you learn today? *(Truths to depend on; promises to believe; warnings to heed; examples to follow / not follow.)*

7. Write these lessons in the form of a question to yourself. *(What should I do? What should I not be doing? Do I truly believe these truths? Do I need to make any changes?)*

DAY 6—BEGIN IN PRAYER

1. Read John 10:1–21.

2. What specific lessons has the Lord taught you or spoken to your heart about this week? Are you willing to allow Him to make the necessary changes in your life?

His sheep hear His voice and follow, how are you doing this week? Are you totally convinced that there is only One Door and have you followed the Good Shepherd through it? Are you experiencing the total freedom and satisfaction in Christ? The warning regarding hirelings applies to every ministry, how are you doing serving the flock? Are you diligently maintaining unity?

Ask the Lord in prayer to make His heart's desire your heart's desire.

3.   Have you completed your memory verse this week? *If not, do so today.*

*The law of his God is in his heart; none of his steps shall slide.
Psalm 37:31*

*I am the good Shepherd: the good Shepherd giveth His life for the
sheep. John 10:11*

DAY 1—BEGIN IN PRAYER

1. Read John 10:22–42.

2. The events in this section of John chapter 10 occurred about 2 months after the discussion described in the previous part of this chapter. What witness did Jesus claim as proof of His deity in these verses?

    a. Verse 25

    b. Verse 27

    c. Verse 30

    d. Verse 36

3. Look up the definition of the following words to give you a better understanding of these Scriptures.

    a. Feast of Dedication (v. 22)

    b. Bear Witness (v. 25)

    c. Follow (v. 27)

    d. Blasphemy (v. 33)

4. Choose a verse to memorize this week. Begin working on it now.

DAY 2—BEGIN IN PRAYER

1. Read John 10:22–42.

2. Re-read John 10:22–26.

3. The Feast of the Dedication, (*Hanukkah: The Feast of Lights*), takes place in December. The feast commemorates the re-dedication of the temple by Judas Maccabeus in 164 B.C., after it had been desecrated by the Antiochus Epiphanes. This conversation is the last of Jesus' public ministry in Jerusalem. What impression do we get from the following references regarding Jesus' attitude toward those who rejected Him and would soon kill Him?

    a. Deuteronomy 5:29

    b. Deuteronomy 32:29

    c. Luke 13:34, 35

    d. Luke 19:41,42

4. The leaders surrounded Jesus in the Temple and demanded, *"if Thou be the Christ, tell us plainly."* Jesus had plainly declared who He was to those who truly wanted to hear. Review the following accounts and record the words of His testimony.

    a. John 1:47–51

    b. John 3:13–15

c. John 4:25, 26

d. John 9:35–38

5. Jesus used His works as a testimony of Who He is. What do the following prophecies of the Old Testament say of the coming Messiah and the works that He would do?

a. Psalm 146:5–9

b. Isaiah 29:18, 19

c. Isaiah 42:6–8

What was the testimony of those who inquired of Jesus whether He was the Messiah?

a. Matthew 11:4–6

6. What specific lessons did you learn today? *(Truths to depend on; promises to believe; warnings to heed; examples to follow / not follow.)*

7. Write these lessons in the form of a question to yourself. *(What should I do? What should I not be doing? Do I truly believe these truths? Do I need to make any changes?)*

DAY 3—BEGIN IN PRAYER

1. Read John 10:22–42.

2. Re-read John 10:27–31.

3. The shepherd and the sheep had an intimate relationship. The shepherd knew the names and the characteristics of the sheep. He cared for them, provided for them, protected them and loved them. Even more does our Heavenly Father care for us, His sheep. What do we learn from these verses regarding the Lord's care for you?

    a. Isaiah 12:2

    b. Isaiah 40:11

    c. Isaiah 41:10

    d. Isaiah 43:2

4. The promise to the sheep of the Lord's flock is eternal life and eternal security. Jesus declared, *"no one can pluck them out of My hand."* When we come to the Lord repenting of our sin and declaring our need for the Savior, we become His by the grace of God. We could not do anything *good enough* to

earn, win or deserve salvation, therefore, we cannot do anything *bad enough* to lose salvation. What strength and comfort can we gain from these Scriptures?

a. Psalm 121:1–8

b. Psalm 138:8

c. Philippians 1:6

d. Jude 24, 25

5.   In verse 30 Jesus answers their question in "plain speech." He declares, *"I and My Father are One."* Jesus was not saying that He and the Father are the same person. The Father and the Son are two persons in the Trinity, but they are one in essence. Given this essential oneness, the Father and Son act as one—what the Father does, the Son does; and vice versa. This is one of the clearest affirmations of Jesus's divinity in the whole Bible. Notice the reaction of the Jewish leaders, they knew exactly what He was saying. This is the third occasion when they threatened to stone Him. True faith in Jesus leaves no room for middle ground. A decision *must* be made regarding Who you believe He is. What do we discover from the following verses?

a. Joshua 24:15

b. Matthew 6:24

c. Matthew 12:30

d. Revelation 3:15–19

6. What specific lessons did you learn today? *(Truths to depend on; promises to believe; warnings to heed; examples to follow / not follow.)*

7. Write these lessons in the form of a question to yourself. *(What should I do? What should I not be doing? Do I truly believe these truths? Do I need to make any changes?)*

DAY 4—BEGIN IN PRAYER

1. Read John 10:22–42.

2. Re-read John 10:32–38.

3. Jesus invited these Jewish leaders again to take a look at the works He did of the Father. He said, if my words are too hard for you to understand, for what works do you stone Me. Some simply will not hear and believe regardless of how much we share. What is our responsibility as believers to the lost in this world?

a. Matthew 5:14–16

b. 2Corinthians 5:18–21

c. Ephesians 5:8

d. Philippians 2:15, 16

4. Jesus uses an argument that appealed to the Jewish leaders. He spoke to them regarding a Scripture from Psalm 82. The Lord had placed great honor upon the position of judge in the Old Testament. The office of judge was ordained by God and cloaked with respect. The picture in Psalm 82 is that of a court where God has assembled the judges of the earth to warn them that they too will be judged someday. Jesus' argument being that if God called human, evil judges "gods," then why should they stone Him for applying the same title to Himself? Record what you learn regarding this term "gods" from the following verses.

a. Psalm 82:1–6

b. Exodus 7:1, 2

5. A very important point that we shouldn't miss in this discussion is that Jesus affirms the inerrancy of the Scriptures, saying *"the Scripture cannot be broken."* As Christians we must believe and depend on the importance, the power and the inerrancy of the Bible. What has the Holy Spirit recorded about God's Word?

a. Psalm 19:7–11

b. Romans 15:4

c. 2Timothy 3:16, 17

d. Hebrews 4:12

6.   What specific lessons did you learn today? *(Truths to depend on; promises to believe; warnings to heed; examples to follow / not follow.)*

7.   Write these lessons in the form of a question to yourself. *(What should I do? What should I not be doing? Do I truly believe these truths? Do I need to make any changes?)*

DAY 5—BEGIN IN PRAYER

1.   Read John 10:22–42.

2.   Re-read John 10:39–42.

3.   This angry mob sought to arrest Jesus and yet they could not because *"His time had not yet come."* We sometimes find that we fear that harm may come to us or our family. What comfort and assurance can we find in the following Scriptures?

a. 2Chronicles 14:11

b. Psalm 118:6

c. Isaiah 41:10

d. Romans 8:31

4.   Jesus went to the east side of the Jordan. This was His last encounter with the Jewish leaders and the residents of Jerusalem until He would enter into the city on Palm Sunday. He spent the next three months in the countryside. There are several incidents that took place during this time that are recorded in the other Gospels. Record a few details of each of the following accounts.

a. Matthew 19:1, 2

b. Matthew 20:29–34

c. Luke 18:15–17

d. Luke 18:31–34

5. The result of Jesus' countryside ministry was that *"many believed on Him there."* Part of the reason for their belief was the testimony of John the Baptist, who was already dead. Sometimes we think that our witness is having no effect on those who hear us. What encouragement do we find in the following references to be a faithful witness even when we don't see the results?

    a. Isaiah 55:11

    b. Luke 19:17

    c. John 4:34–38

    d. Colossians 3:17, 23

6. What specific lessons did you learn today? *(Truths to depend on; promises to believe; warnings to heed; examples to follow / not follow.)*

7. Write these lessons in the form of a question to yourself. *(What should I do? What should I not be doing? Do I truly believe these truths? Do I need to make any changes?)*

DAY 6—BEGIN IN PRAYER

1. Read John 10:22–42.

2. What specific lessons has the Lord taught you this week? Allow Him to make any necessary changes in your heart today. *(Do not "hear and not do.")*

    Reflect on James 1:22–25. *Be a doer!*

3. Have you completed your memory verse this week? *If not, do so today.*

    My sheep hear My voice, and I know them, and they follow Me: And I give unto them eternal life; and they shall never perish, neither shall any man pluck them out of My hand. John 10:27–28

DAY 1—BEGIN IN PRAYER

1.   Read John 11:1–44.

2.   Up to this point in John's Gospel Jesus has presented Himself as the giver of life to various people. Record His proclamation in each of the verses we have previously studied.

     a. John 3:16

     b. John 4:14

     c. John 6:35

     d. John 8:12

     e. John 10:10, 11

3.   In the account of this seventh *"sign,"* Jesus is *"life"* in its ultimate expression—He is *"the resurrection and the life."* In the face of the tremendous miracle those who looked on had to make a decision regarding "Who" Jesus was (and is). Jesus used this miracle to establish or strengthen the faith of several different groups of people, who were they?

     a. Verses 13–15

b. Verses 20–32

c. Verses 41, 42

4. Choose a verse to memorize this week. *(Don't neglect this important part of your studies!)* Begin working on it now.

DAY 2—BEGIN IN PRAYER

1. Read John 11:1–44.

2. Read John 11:1–13.

3. Although John doesn't introduce Mary, Martha and Lazarus until this late in Jesus' ministry, they were very good friends and Jesus spent much time with them when He was in Jerusalem. They sent for Jesus to let Him know that Lazarus was very near death. The truth is that being close to Jesus doesn't prevent tragedy or suffering from touching your life. Every trial has a purpose and can bring glory to God and show us where our faith needs to grow. How do the following verses effect your outlook on trials?

    a. Romans 5:3–5

    b. Hebrews 12:4–11

    c. 1 Peter 1:6, 7

d. James 1:2–4

4. Jesus *loved (agapao)* Martha, Mary and Lazarus. This *agape* love is the highest kind of love—not just affection, but love that *results from a moral choice; not swayed by emotion; fully unconditional.* There is nothing that we can do to earn this love. It is the very character and nature of God. Yet, Jesus allowed Mary and Martha to wait for God's perfect timing in this situation. The Scriptures are full of instructions on waiting on the Lord, ask your Father to increase your ability to wait for His timing.

a. Psalm 33:20–22

b. Psalm 40:1–3

c. Isaiah 25:9

d. Lamentations 3:25, 26

5. Jesus mentioned returning to Judea and the first thoughts of the disciples were of the impending danger from the Jewish leaders. As children of the Lord, we need to be reminded, as were the disciples, that nothing can harm us unless it is in the Father's will and His timing. Jesus did not fear man and He knew that He must do the work of the Father while there was still time (light). We need to be about our Father's business as we wait for the Lord's return. What encouragement do you find in the following verses to serve while there is still light?

a. Romans 13:12–14

b. Ephesians 5:14–18

c. Colossians 2:6, 7

d. 1 Thessalonians 5:5–8

6. What specific lessons did you learn today? *(Truths to depend on; promises to believe; warnings to heed; examples to follow / not follow.)*

7. Write these lessons in the form of a question to yourself. *(What should I do? What should I not be doing? Do I truly believe these truths? Do I need to make any changes?)*

DAY 3—BEGIN IN PRAYER

1. Read John 11:1–44.

2. Re-read John 11:14–27.

3. Jesus spoke to the disciples regarding Lazarus saying that he was *"asleep."* When they did not understand what He was telling them He clearly said, *"Lazarus is dead."* He was glad, not that Lazarus had died or that Mary and Martha had suffered, but that because of the miracle, their faith would be strengthened. Lazarus died so that Jesus could show His power over death. What declaration had Jesus previously made to claim His power over death?

a. John 5:21

b. John 6:40; 54

c. John 10:17, 18

d. John 10:27, 28

4. Bethany was approximately two miles away from Jerusalem. Many of the Jews had come to comfort Mary and Martha. Now four days after Lazarus' death Jesus arrives. Martha rushed out to meet Jesus and declares, *"if You had been here, my brother would not have died."* How often we think that we know exactly what is the best answer for every situation. This was not the case for Martha nor is it for us. What truths do we learn about God and His plans for our life?

a. Psalm 40:5

b. Isaiah 55:8, 9

c. Jeremiah 29:11

d. Romans 8:28

5. Jesus offers the reassurance to Martha that her brother will rise again. She has this hope but believes that this resurrection is far off in the future. Re-read John 11:25, 26, *do you believe this?* Jesus again proclaims: *"I AM the resurrection and the life."* What effect does the truth of the resurrection have on your life today?

    a. 1Corinthians 15:20–26

    b. 1Corinthians 15:53–57

    c. Philippians 3:10–14

    d. Philippians 3:20, 21

6. What specific lessons did you learn today? *(Truths to depend on; promises to believe; warnings to heed; examples to follow / not follow.)*

7. Write these lessons in the form of a question to yourself. *(What should I do? What should I not be doing? Do I truly believe these truths? Do I need to make any changes?)*

DAY 4—BEGIN IN PRAYER *(Don't Neglect Your Teacher!)*

1. Read John 11:1–44.

2. Read John 11:28–35.

3. Martha lost no time in running back to tell Mary that Jesus was coming. Mary rushed to meet Him and when she got there she did what was characteristic of Mary's devotion, *"she fell down at His feet."* Where do we find Mary on the other occasions that she is mentioned in the Bible?

    a. Luke 10:39

    b. John 12:3

4. Mary echoed the statement of Martha, *"if you would have been here..."* How often we fall short in the faith and willingness to trust God with our lives and the lives of our families. What can we do to strengthen our faith and trust in the Lord?

    a. 1 Chronicles 16:11–14

    b. Matthew 11:28–30

c. Matthew 16:24, 25

d. Ephesians 6:16–18

5. When Jesus saw the *weeping (wailing, extreme passionate expressions of grief)* of Mary and the Jews *"He groaned in His Spirit and was troubled (deeply agitated)* and *"He wept."* There are a number of *opinions* about the reason for this reaction from Jesus: in sympathy for those He loved; the result of sin on mankind; the unbelief of those who looked on or maybe because He was going to bring Lazarus back from eternity. What is true is that Jesus knows and has experienced the pain, the heartache, the loneliness and the temptation of this world. He knows exactly where you hurt and suffer and is there to meet you and keep you through it. Use the following references to remind you of His love for you.

a. Deuteronomy 7:7–9

b. Jeremiah 31:3

c. Hebrews 2:17, 18

d. Hebrews 4:14, 15

6. What specific lessons did you learn today? *(Truths to depend on; promises to believe; warnings to heed; examples to follow / not follow.)*

7. Write these lessons in the form of a question to yourself. *(What should I do? What should I not be doing? Do I truly believe these truths? Do I need to make any changes?)*

DAY 5—BEGIN IN PRAYER

1. Read John 11:1–44.

2. Re-read John 11:36–44.

3. At the beginning of this chapter Mary, Martha and the crowd came with conditional belief. They thought that Jesus could have prevented the death of Lazarus *if* He had been there. There were still many in this crowd who doubted and they were about to see the mighty hand of God at work. Is there *anything* too hard for God?

    a. Genesis 18:14

    b. Jeremiah 32:17; 26, 27

    c. Luke 1:37

    d. Luke 18:27

4. Is there anything *too hard for God* in your life today? Be reminded of His faithfulness through these Scriptures that are written just for *you*.

    a. Psalm 84:11, 12

    b. Micah 7:7, 8

    c. Philippians 4:19

    d. 2Corinthians 9:8–11

5. The purpose of this miracle and all the others that Jesus performed was *"for the glory of God, that the Son of God would be glorified,"* (John 11:4). The purpose of our lives, as believers, is exactly the same. We are here to bring glory to our Father by everything we say and do. Jesus used those who looked on to assist in this miracle by moving the stone and unwrapping the grave clothes and so will He use us to bring Him honor and glory as we surrender our lives to Him.

    a. Matthew 5:16

    b. John 15:8–11

    c. 1Peter 2:9–12

d. 1Peter 4:11–14

6. What specific lessons did you learn today? *(Truths to depend on; promises to believe; warnings to heed; examples to follow / not follow.)*

7. Write these lessons in the form of a question to yourself. *(What should I do? What should I not be doing? Do I truly believe these truths? Do I need to make any changes?)*

DAY 6—BEGIN IN PRAYER

1. Read John 11:1–44.

2. *What specific lessons has the Lord taught you this week? Is there any area of your faith that is conditional? Will you surrender it to the Lord? Does God's timing seem to be too late, in your opinion? You can trust Him with every area of your life. Does your life bring honor and glory to God when He is the only One Who is looking?*

Read Colossians 3:17 and use it as a measuring stick this week.

3.   Have you completed your memory verse this week? *If, not do so today.*

Jesus said unto her, I am the resurrection, and the life: he that believeth in Me, though he were dead, yet shall he live: And whosoever liveth and believeth in Me shall never die. Believest thou this? John 11:25, 26

DAY 1—BEGIN IN PRAYER

1. Read John 11:45–57.

2. Read Matthew chapters 19–20. (This is a partial account of Jesus' ministry outside of Jerusalem during this period which is not covered in John's Gospel. Luke gives us even more details in: Luke 13:10 – 19:28.)

3. Jealousy and rage had taken deep root in the hearts to these leaders and it caused their eyes to be totally blinded to the truth. Record their decision from verse 53 and then read Isaiah 53:1–12. *How does this effect your outlook on your life today?*

4. Choose a verse to memorize this week. Begin working on it today.

DAY 2—BEGIN IN PRAYER

1. Read John 11:45–57.

2. Re-read John 11:45–50.

3. The results of Lazarus being raised from the dead by Jesus brought again a division among the people. We would think that everyone who witnessed the event would believe. Read Luke 16:19–31, what do we learn about miracles and their effect on faith?

4. Some believed (at least that Jesus could do this miracle) and others went immediately to tell the Pharisees. This news brought panic to those who carried all the power, religious and political. The Sanhedrin, which was the high court, was lead by the high priest. They gathered now with their rivals,

the Pharisees. What they feared was the loss of their power and position and the driving force behind their actions was pride. What do we learn about pride? *How has it kept you from seeing the truth?*

a. Psalm 10:4

b. Psalm 73:6

c. Proverbs 16:18

d. 1John 2:16

5.   Caiaphas, the high priest, was appointed by Rome. This office was originally a position that was ordained by God but it had long since become a political position held by those who did not even consider the Lord. Caiaphas spoke a word of prophecy regarding the death of Jesus. The Lord is very capable to use any means to speak His truths. Remember Balaam's donkey? What does God's Word teach us regarding human kings and leaders?

a. Psalm 75:6, 7

b. Proverbs 21:1

c. 1Chronicles 29:11, 12

d. Romans 13:1–6

6. What specific lessons did you learn today? *(Truths to depend on; promises to believe; warnings to heed; examples to follow / not follow.)*

7. Write these lessons in the form of a question to yourself. *(What should I do? What should I not be doing? Do I truly believe these truths? Do I need to make any changes?)*

DAY 3—BEGIN IN PRAYER

1. Read John 11:45–57.

2. Re-read John 11:51–54.

3. John gives us the commentary on this prophecy of Caiaphas, that he spoke not of himself. The truth was that Jesus would die for the nation and even more that He would gather together, as one, the children of God. It was for this purpose that Jesus came. He was born to die. What reminders and thanksgiving come from the truth in the following Scriptures?

   a. Mark 10:45

   b. 2Corinthians 5:21

c. Philippians 2:5–8

d. 1 Peter 1:18–21

4. As believers in Jesus Christ we are called together as *one*. Unity is often spoken of in the church yet it is not necessarily always practiced. We **are one** but it is our responsibility to practice, guard and protect that unity. What direction do we find regarding our unity in these verses?

a. John 17:20–23

b. Romans 15:5, 6

c. 1 Corinthians 1:10

d. Ephesians 4:1–3

5. Now, from this day forth, they took counsel together to put Him to death. They decided that it was best to rid themselves of Jesus to save the people but what they didn't know was that they were rejecting their only hope of salvation.

In about 40 years the Romans would conquer and destroy Israel and the people would be dispersed for over 1,800 years. They believed that they could win. They couldn't. Man cannot frustrate the plan of God. They can oppose Him—but they will lose. God is Sovereign—nothing or no one can frustrate His plans. *What comfort and peace do you find knowing that you are His child?*

a. Deuteronomy 32:39–44

b. Isaiah 45:5–9

c. Isaiah 45:18–22

d. John 10:27, 28

6. What specific lessons did you learn today? *(Truths to depend on; promises to believe; warnings to heed; examples to follow / not follow.)*

7. Write these lessons in the form of a question to yourself. *(What should I do? What should I not be doing? Do I truly believe these truths? Do I need to make any changes?)*

DAY 4—BEGIN IN PRAYER

1. Read Matthew 19–20. *(This isn't a mistake.)*

2. Re-read Matthew 19–20 slowly and write down any specific areas or attitudes that the Lord is dealing with in your life. Share one area with your group, if you feel like you can.

3. God would greatly desire to make these changes in your life. *Will you allow Him to work?* Spend some extra time in prayer for these areas and your family today.

DAY 5—BEGIN IN PRAYER

(Remember there is no learning without a Teacher!)

1. Read John 11:45–57.

2. Re-read John 11:55–57.

3. Notice that John says the Jew's Passover was at hand. This is the third Passover Feast mentioned in John. Jesus' time had almost come. The historical records of Josephus says that 250,000 lambs were sacrificed on this Passover in 30 A.D. One for every household (extended family), which means that there could have been 2.5 million people in Jerusalem.

    They came to purify themselves through the Old Covenant and would come face-to-face with the New Covenant. Record what you learn about the New Covenant.

    a. Jeremiah 31:31–33

    b. Matthew 26:28

    c. Hebrews 8:12, 13

    d. Hebrews 9:15, 16

4. The curious spectators wondered whether He would come. Isn't it the same today, that many watch from the gallery not willing to be totally committed to faith in Jesus Christ. What level of dedication and commitment are we to devote to Jesus, Who is our Lord and Savior?

   a. Matthew 16:24, 25

   b. Mark 12:32, 33

   c. Luke 14:33

   d. Galatians 2:20

5. This was the very reason that Jesus had come into the world. This would be the last Passover Feast that had any significance. The last sacrifice would be offered once and for all. The chief priest and the Pharisees, driven by the enemy, were ready and willing to kill an innocent man. His blood was shed for my sins and yours. Read and meditate on this awesome truth. *Does it cause your heart to rejoice?*

   a. Romans 5:6–8

   b. Romans 8:3, 4

   c. Titus 2:13, 14

d. 1Peter 3:18

6.   What specific lessons did you learn today? *(Truths to depend on, promises to believe, warnings to heed, examples to follow / not follow.)*

7.   Write these lessons in the form of a question to yourself. *(What should I do? What should I not be doing? Do I truly believe these truths? Do I need to make any changes?)*

DAY 6—BEGIN IN PRAYER

1.   Read John 11:45–57.

2.   What specific lessons has the Lord spoken to you about this week?

*Has pride or jealousy ever blinded you from seeing the truth? Do you fear the state of the nation or world? God is Sovereign, do you truly believe its true? Are you diligently defending the unity of the Body? How would you rate your commitment and devotion to the Lord? (Lukewarm is **not good**— **Revelation 3:16**.) Spend time in prayer today handing these areas over to the Lord for His work to be accomplished.*

3.   Have you completed your memory verse this week? *If not, do it today.*

And this spake he not of himself: but being high priest that year, he prophesied that Jesus should die for that nation; And not for that nation only, but that also he should gather together in one the children of God that were scattered abroad. John 11:51, 52

DAY 1—BEGIN IN PRAYER

1. Read John 12:1–19.

2. Re-read John 12:1–19 and list a few details of the two events we will be studying this week.

    a. John 12:1–11

    b. John 12:12–19

3. What aspects of the Christian life do we find represented by each of the lives of those who followed and loved Jesus in Bethany?

    a. Martha (v. 2)

    b. Mary (v. 3)

    c. Lazarus (vs. 10, 11)

4. Choose a verse to memorize this week. Begin working on it today.

DAY 2—BEGIN IN PRAYER

1. Read John 12:1–19.

2. Re-read John 12:1–11.

3. Remember in John 11:54 that Jesus walked no more among the Jews openly for they sought to kill Him and now He is back in Bethany only 6 days before the Passover. He truly loved Mary, Martha and Lazarus and had intimate fellowship with them. He loves you equally and desires the same intimate fellowship with you. What direction do we gain from looking at Jesus' prayer life and His intimacy with the Father that we should use as a pattern?

a. Matthew 14:23

b. Mark 1:35

c. Mark 6:46

d. Luke 6:12

4. Martha gives us a model of service in the life of the believer and something has definitely changed in her attitude. No more complaining or whining. She was serving from the heart. *Is your serving like the old Martha or this one? How are we to serve?*

a. Jeremiah 24:7

b. Ephesians 6:5–8

c. Philippians 2:12–15

d. Colossians 3:22–24

5. Mary gives us the example of self-sacrificing worship. What do we learn about true worship and what does it require of our lives?

   a. Psalm 29:2

   b. Isaiah 66:1, 2

   c. Mark 12:30

   d. John 4:23, 24

6. What specific lessons did you learn today? *(Truths to depend on; promises to believe; warnings to heed; examples to follow / not follow.)*

7. Write these lessons in the form of a question to yourself. *(What should I do? What should I not be doing? Do I truly believe these truths? Do I need to make any changes?)*

DAY 3—BEGIN IN PRAYER

1. Read John 12:1–19.

2. Re-read John 12:1–11. *(Same as yesterday!)*

3. Sometimes when we seek to serve the Lord we are met with major criticism. The Lord desires only that we are faithful and willing to do our very best for Him. Read the Parable of the Talents in Matthew 25:14–30. What response was given to the servant with five talents and the servant with two talents? *Is there an area that requires more faithful attention in your life?*

4. In the case of Judas, what are we told was the *real* source of the complaint (v. 6)?

    We need to be careful not to be tripped up by sin in using *righteous reasons* to mask our selfishness, greed or jealousy. We need to examine our own heart and motives so that we will be honest before the Lord. What do we learn about spiritual self-examination from the following Scriptures?

    a. Proverbs 16:1–3

    b. 1 Corinthians 11:28

    c. 2 Corinthians 13:4–6

d. 1John 3:18–22

5.   Lazarus' life was a living witness and simply being that witness made Him a target for those who hated Jesus. What warning and comfort do we find when we face alienation or suffering (or death in some parts of the world) because we follow Jesus?

a. Matthew 5:10–12

b. Romans 8:17,18

c. Philippians 1:27–30

d. 2Timothy 3:12

6.   What specific lessons did you learn today? *(Truths to depend on; promises to believe; warnings to heed; examples to follow / not follow.)*

7.   Write these lessons in the form of a question to yourself. *(What should I do? What should I not be doing? Do I truly believe these truths? Do I need to make any changes?)*

DAY 4—BEGIN IN PRAYER

1. Read John 12:1–19.

2. Re-read John 12:12–19.

3. In the raising of Lazarus from the dead we saw that even the most miraculous events will not convince some to believe. In the account to the Triumphal Entry we see that the fulfilling of prophecy makes not even a dent in the hardened hearts of the enemies of the Lord. John's description of the Triumphal Entry, mentioned in all four Gospels, is the shortest account. Read this account recorded in the other three Gospels and record any new details you find.

    a. Matthew 21:1–11

    b. Mark 11:1–11

    c. Luke 19:28–40

4. As the crowd began to gather they shouted, *"Hosanna,"* which is the equivalent of saying, *"Save Now!"* They thought that their conquering King had finally come to liberate them from Roman rule. They were looking for a conquering King (and He will be) but they missed the prophecy of the suffering Messiah that was to die for the people. The Palm branches symbolized victory to the Jews and certainly Jesus was about to have victory over the enemy. However, that victory would come through intense suffering. What reminders do we find in the following references of Jesus' suffering?

    a. Isaiah 53:4, 5

    b. Hebrews 9:28

c. 1 Peter 2:21–25

4. 1 Peter 3:18

5. Along with the shouted greeting, the people chanted an ancient blessing from the Psalms. Read Psalm 118:25–26. The Passover celebration made use of the "Hallel" section of the Psalms (113–118), singing them as hymns of worship. Choose one of these Psalms and use it today to worship the Lord, Who willingly made this entry into the city where He would die for you and me.

6. What specific lessons did you learn today? *(Truths to depend on; promises to believe; warnings to heed; examples to follow / not follow.)*

7. Write these lessons in the form of a question to yourself. *(What should I do? What should I not be doing? Do I truly believe these truths? Do I need to make any changes?)*

DAY 5—BEGIN IN PRAYER

1. Read John 12:1–19.

2. Re-read John 12:12–19. *(Again!)*

3. This entrance into Jerusalem was prophesied by the prophet Zechariah. Write out the prophecy from Zechariah 9:9. What image do you get of a King riding on a donkey?

In this coming, Israel's King would be a humble servant, not a conqueror. He would not be exalted to a throne, but lifted up on a cross. Use the following Scriptures as a reminder of His humility in being willing to lay down His life for us. What instruction is given for us to follow?

a. Matthew 20:27, 28

b. Luke 22:26, 27

c. John 13:4–16

d. Philippians 2:5–8

4. Notice that even the disciples did not understand all that was happening and why. But after the resurrection it became much clearer. We do not, and will not, have all the answers or total understanding in our lives, but we are called to trust our Father in Heaven. *Is there an area in your life that you don't understand and yet need to entrust to your Heavenly Father?* What encouragement do you find in the following verses?

a. Psalm 65:4

b. Proverbs 3:5, 6

c. Isaiah 43:1–3

d. Matthew 6:31–34

5. The Pharisees were very concerned about the *perceived* popularity of Jesus. Unfortunately, in only a few days many who praised Jesus would be crying, *"Crucify Him."* Words are not enough to bring salvation. Professing faith is not the same as possessing salvation. What is the proof of a true believer?

a. Matthew 24:13

b. John 8:31

c. Hebrews 3:6

d. Hebrews 3:14

6. What specific lessons did you learn today? *(Truths to depend on; promises to believe; warnings to heed; examples to follow / not follow.)*

7. Write these lessons in the form of a question to yourself. *(What should I do? What should I not be doing? Do I truly believe these truths? Do I need to make any changes?)*

DAY 6—BEGIN IN PRAYER

1. Read John 12:1–19.

2. What specific lessons has the Lord taught you this week. Review your answers to questions #6–#7 of each day. What is the Lord requesting you to surrender to Him? *Will you let Him have your whole life?*

3. Have you completed your memory verse this week? *If not, do so today.*

Then said Jesus, Let her alone: against the day of My burying hath she kept this. John 12:7

DAY 1—BEGIN IN PRAYER

1. Read John 12:20–50.

2. Re-read John 12:20–50. We find that *"the hour is come."* The *"hour"* was the moment for both Jesus and the Father to be glorified. What events were going to glorify the Father and the Son?

    a. John 12:24

    b. John 12:30–33

3. Look up the definitions of the following words for a deeper understanding of their meanings. (Be sure to take your definitions back into the context of the verses they are from.)

    a. Loves (v. 25)

    b. Lose (v. 25)

    c. Glorify (v. 28)

    d. Hardened (v. 40)

    e. Praise (v. 43)

    f. Reject (v. 48)

Jesus
CHRIST
son of GOD

4. Choose a verse to memorize this week. Begin working on it today.

DAY 2—BEGIN IN PRAYER

1. Read John 12:20–50.

2. Re-read John 12:20–26.

3. In this last section that we are studying, Jesus explains to His listeners (and us) why He must die. There were certain Greeks who sought to personally meet Jesus. We are never told whether they got this audience, but we can be sure that the teaching and instruction that follows was initiated by this request. It gives a clear picture of the universal truth of the Gospel. *"Whosoever will come"* is invited to come to Jesus and *"He will in no wise cast them out."* What do we learn about the universal call to Jesus?

    a. Mark 16:15, 16

    b. Luke 24:46, 47

    c. Romans 10:12, 13

4. The hour had come that the Son of Man was to be "glorified." We would think that Jesus might say "crucified" but His eyes were on the eternal, not the physical. (Do not forget, however, that Jesus was fully man and the suffering He was about to face was tremendous. The physical pain, the humiliation and the agony of sinless God becoming sin and being separated from the Father caused Him great heartache.) What details do you find about God being glorified?

    a. Isaiah 53:10–12

b. Isaiah 55:1–5

c. John 17:1–5; 9, 10

d. Luke 23:46, 47

5. This statement, prefaced by the *"Verily, verily,"* gives solemn emphasis and enforces a great truth. The grain of wheat may remain in the granary for a thousand years and be preserved, but it is useless there. It neither reproduces, nor is food. It is when it falls into the ground and undergoes dissolution, that it brings forth fruit. It is fruitful by giving itself up. So, too, Christ must give Himself up. His death was needful in order that He might impart life to the nation. There is a lesson here for disciples who would *"bear much fruit."* What do we learn about our need to *"die"* to be fruitful?

a. Matthew 16:24–26

b. Romans 6:6–8

c. 2Corinthians 4:8–11

d. Galatians 2:20

6. What specific lessons did you learn today? *(Truths to depend on; promises to believe; warnings to heed; examples to follow / not follow.)*

7. Write these lessons in the form of a question to yourself. *(What should I do? What should I not be doing? Do I truly believe these truths? Do I need to make any changes?)*

DAY 3—BEGIN IN PRAYER

1. Read John 12:20–50.

2. Re-read John 12:27–36.

3. Jesus declared: *"Now is my soul troubled,"* this is the only indication recorded in John that Jesus was troubled by the approaching hour. He declares, *"Father, glorify your name."* This is the third time God had now spoken audibly from heaven. Record the details of the other two times. What do you think may have been the reason for these occasions?

    a. Matthew 3:16, 17

    b. Matthew 17:1–5

4. This was the hour for which Jesus had come into the world, the hour of the cross; it was to be the hour of judgment, the crisis, which should determine who should rule the world. The cross became a throne. It gave Him the crown. Now shall the prince of this world be cast out. The cross cast him out, and

dethroned him; he is now a usurper and shall finally be cast into the lake of fire. What further details and encouragement do you find in these Scriptures about the judgment of the prince of this world?

a. John 16:8–11

b. Ephesians 2:1–3

c. Colossians 2:13–15

d. Revelation 20:2, 3; 10

5. Jesus again uses that description of light and darkness. Those who were listening sought again to argue. He told them there was only a little while and their opportunity for faith would be gone. His instruction to us is, *"while you have light, believe in the light, that you may be children of the light." Are you a child of the light?* How ought you to be living? *How are you doing?*

a. Romans 13:12–14

b. Ephesians 5:1–10

c. 1 John 1:7

d. 1John 2:9, 10

6.　What specific lessons did you learn today? *(Truths to depend on; promises to believe; warnings to heed; examples to follow / not follow.)*

7.　Write these lessons in the form of a question to yourself. *(What should I do? What should I not be doing? Do I truly believe these truths? Do I need to make any changes?)*

DAY 4—BEGIN IN PRAYER

1.　Read John 12:20–50.

2.　Re-read John 12:37–43.

3.　They *would not* believe so because of the hardness of their hearts they *could not* believe. They deliberately, persistently rejected Him. Only thirty-six miracles are recorded in the Gospels, but the phrases *"so many,"* and *"many other signs"* are used to describe the miracles of the Lord. Some will not hear so God hardens their hearts, so they cannot believe. What do we learn about this dangerous position?

a. Genesis 6:3

b. Romans 1:28–32

c. 2Peter 2:12–15

d. Revelation 22:10, 11

4. There were some among the chief rulers that believed on Jesus, but the cost of following Him was too high. We are called to follow whole-heartedly with our whole life. What example do we find in the following verses? *Is their anything too costly in your life compared to the sacrifice paid on your behalf?*

    a. Matthew 10:37, 38

    b. Luke 14:26–33

    c. Luke 18:18–24

    d. Acts 20:23, 24

5. These secret believers loved the praises of men more than the praises of God. What does God's Word tell us about the love of this world and the things that belong to it?

    a. John 15:18, 19

b. Romans 12:2

c. Galatians 1:10

d. 1John 2:15–17

6.   What specific lessons did you learn today? *(Truths to depend on; promises to believe; warnings to heed; examples to follow / not follow.)*

7.   Write these lessons in the form of a question to yourself. *(What should I do? What should I not be doing? Do I truly believe these truths? Do I need to make any changes?)*

DAY 5—BEGIN IN PRAYER

1.   Read John 12:20–50.

2.   Re-read John 12:44–50.

3.   John closes this section of his gospel about Jesus' public ministry with a summary of Jesus' entire testimony. It is an ultimatum set before the crowds and the world today: Believe in Jesus, the Light of the World, or live in darkness under God's judgment. In many places in Scripture the realm of God and the realm of evil are contrasted by the differences between light and darkness. Record the stark differences between the two.

a. Isaiah 9:2

b. John 1:4, 5, 9

c. Acts 26:18

d. Romans 13:12–14

e. 2Corinthians 4:6

f. Ephesians 5:8–11

g. Ephesians 6:12, 13

h. Colossians 1:12–14

i. 1John 1:5, 7

j. 1John 2:8–11

6. What specific lessons did you learn today? *(Truths to depend on; promises to believe; warnings to heed; examples to follow / not follow.)*

7. Write these lessons in the form of a question to yourself. *(What should I do? What should I not be doing? Do I truly believe these truths? Do I need to make any changes?)*

DAY 6—BEGIN IN PRAYER

1. Read John 12:30–50.

2. What specific lessons or specific areas of your life and heart has the Lord been speaking to you about this week? Spend some time in prayer today asking Him to make the needed changes in you life. *(Be specific in your prayer.)*

3. Have you completed your memory verse this week? *If not, do so today.*

4. For next week: Re-read John 1–12.

> *If any man serve Me, let him follow Me; and where I am, there shall also My servant be: if any man serve Me, him will My Father honour. John 12:26*

You made it—Praise the Lord! I'm certain that you have grown tremendously. It's a promise. To continue your study of the Gospel of John, purchase John Part 2 from the Chapel Store at Morningstar Christian Chapel or through the online store at www.growingthrugrace.com.

All scripture is given by inspiration of God, and is profitable for doctrine, for reproof, for correction, for instruction in righteousness: That the man of God may be perfect, thoroughly furnished unto all good works. 2Timothy 3:16, 17

Made in the USA
Middletown, DE
15 May 2021